DON'T LEAD LIKE A JERK

HOW TO LEAD PEOPLE, DRIVE PROFIT, AND ACTUALLY GET STUFF DONE

KARLIE CREMIN

AWARD-WINNING LEADERSHIP EXPERT

TABLE OF CONTENTS

FOREWORD v

INTRODUCTION vii

CHAPTER 1: Why Leadership is Broken (and What We've
Been Getting Wrong)... 1

CHAPTER 2: The Dynamic Leader Framework: People, Proficiency
and Profit.. 15

CHAPTER 3: How to Lead People (and not lose your
mind doing it) 41

CHAPTER 4: Getting Stuff Done Without the Drama.................... 65

CHAPTER 5: Profit: Making the Work Actually Pay Off 89

CHAPTER 6: Staying Out of the Three D's 111

CHAPTER 7: The Science of Great (and Terrible) Leadership 121

CHAPTER 8: The Dynamic Leader Toolkit 137

CHAPTER 9: The Future Won't Wait for Better Bosses 153

About the Author: 161

FOREWORD

When I started in leadership work, I thought the job was about plans, strategies and numbers.

It turned out to be about people. People with ambitions, with families, with allergies to corporate buzzwords, with dreams that don't fit neatly into a quarterly plan.

Over the years I've sat across from leaders at every level - the first-time supervisor who's terrified of their first difficult conversation, the CEO who can't sleep because the board wants growth yesterday, the brilliant technical expert who's suddenly in charge of other humans and wondering if they made a huge mistake.

I've seen the same patterns repeat: most leaders don't set out to be jerks. They get promoted, overloaded, under-supported, and fall back on habits that accidentally turn them into the boss they swore they'd never be.

Writing this book wasn't on my to-do list when I started DLPA (Dynamic Leadership Programs Australia). But after years of seeing the same mistakes - and the same light-bulb moments when someone realises they can lead better - I wanted to put those stories, tools and a little humour in one place.

This book is part field-guide, part mirror, part pep-talk. It's written for anyone who has ever stared at their calendar and wondered when the actual leading part of their leadership job is supposed to happen.

If you came here expecting another sterile leadership manual, I'm sorry (but also not sorry).

I wanted to write something that sounds like the conversations I have with real leaders in real rooms.

You'll meet some of them in these pages - Dave, Maya, Marcus, Renee. They're real in all the ways that matter, even if a few details have been changed. You'll hear about the science that explains why some teams thrive and others slowly unravel, and you'll get practical tools that don't require a PhD or a 3-day offsite to use.

Most of all, I hope you'll feel like you have a guide who knows the terrain - the late-night email panic, the budget squeeze, the joy of watching a team finally click.

Thank you for picking up Don't Lead Like a Jerk.

Here's to a world with fewer jerks, more dynamic leaders, and maybe a few more nights where everyone gets to go home on time.

– Karlie Cremin

CEO, DLPA (Dynamic Leadership Programs Australia)

INTRODUCTION

You Know That Boss

If you've been in the workforce for more than about five minutes, you've met them:

The boss who thought the title automatically made them brilliant - and would like you to know about it.

That's the same one who called "urgent" meetings that could have been an email, or could have waited until next week. The one who thought feedback meant throwing a grenade into the meeting and walking off.

Maybe you laughed about them over Friday night drinks. Maybe you still wake up thinking of that time they made you redo the presentation at 10 p.m. because they "didn't like the vibe of slide seven."

Or maybe, just maybe... you've caught yourself doing something just as bad.

Before you start feeling defensive, know this: I've been there too. Every leader has a jerk moment - sometimes two or more. It usually happens somewhere between the second coffee of the morning and the fifth Zoom call of the day. The trick is to notice it, laugh at it, and fix it before your team starts updating their résumés and adding 'Open to Work' to their LinkedIn.

The Three D's of Terrible Leadership

Over two decades of consulting, and in starting my own business Dynamic Leadership Programs Australia (DLPA) I started to see the same patterns pop up, no matter the industry: construction, government, professional services, car-rental depots, you name it.

Most struggling leaders can be filed under one of the Three D's:

Dormant: technically employed, mentally retired. They're just going through the motions, never really getting stuff done.

Distant: busy writing strategy documents in a corner office while the team quietly unravels.

Disaster: charismatic chaos merchants. They energise a room and then set it on fire.

You've probably worked for at least one of them. If you haven't, congratulations - but don't get too smug, because odds are you've had a few Dormant or Distant (maybe even Disastrous) moments yourself.

Why We Keep Getting It Wrong

We're not born knowing how to lead people.

We promote the top salesperson, the best engineer, the longest-serving staff member and then expect them to instinctively know how to run a team. We hand over a laptop, a shiny new title, maybe an org-chart update, and wish them luck.

If we treated any other skill like that - say, flying a plane - no one would ever get on board. But somehow we think leadership will just... happen.

It doesn't.

Leadership is a skill. A learnable, improvable, practical skill - but only if we stop pretending it's about charisma or PowerPoint slides.

Enter the DLPA Model

After working with hundreds of organisations and thousands of leaders, we at DLPA figured out why some leaders thrive and others flame out.

It comes down to three pillars:

People – Leading humans, not job titles. Building trust, culture, resilience.

Proficiency – Knowing what you're doing and being able to execute it well.

Profit – Making sure all that effort actually creates sustainable results for the business.

When a leader gets all three right, we call them Dynamic Leaders. When they don't, we get the Three D's - Dormant, Distant, or Disaster.

Think of it like a three-legged stool: kick out one leg and it all wobbles.

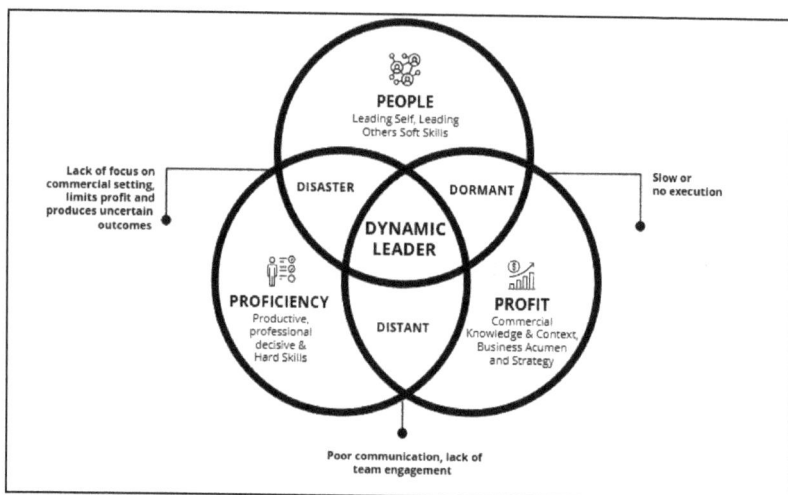

Not Another Textbook

If you're expecting a neat corporate manual with bullet-point platitudes, this is not that book.

There's enough leadership-speak out there to tranquilise a rhino in under three pages.

This book is written the way I facilitate workshops:

- Straight-talking.
- A bit cheeky.
- Plenty of real-world stories (some flattering, some not).
- Exercises you can actually do, not just highlight in yellow.

Leadership is hard enough - the least we can do is laugh while we figure it out.

A Few Stories You'll Hear

You'll hear about the project manager who could quote every policy but hadn't spoken to her team in weeks. The site foreman who thought shouting was a motivational strategy... until his best welder quit mid-shift. The finance director who learned more about influence from coaching his daughter's netball team than from any MBA lecture.

These stories aren't here to shame anyone. They're here to remind us that leadership isn't theory; it's human, messy, funny, and fixable.

Why Bother Changing?

Because people don't leave companies - they leave jerks. And every time a good employee quits, it costs money, morale, and momentum. A leader who can connect with people, get the work done, and keep an eye on the bigger picture is worth their weight in gold (and fewer HR complaints).

What You'll Get Out of This Book

By the last page, you'll know how to:

- Lead humans without losing your sense of humour or your mind.
- Build a team that trusts you enough to tell you the truth.
- Balance empathy with accountability so you're not the "nice but useless" boss.
- Understand the commercial side of leadership so your great culture actually funds itself.

- Avoid being remembered at your farewell party as "that jerk boss."

A Note to the Jerk in All of Us

This isn't a witch-hunt.

We've all snapped in a meeting, ignored feedback, written an email we regretted or found ourselves over our heads. The point isn't to feel guilty; it's to get and be better.

If you're already a decent leader, we'll sharpen your edge. If you've got a few jerk-ish habits, we'll help you swap them for ones that work. Either way, you'll finish this book with a clearer head, a sturdier toolkit, and maybe a few new jokes.

Let's Get to Work

Leadership is too important to leave to chance - and far too human and nuanced to be taught like accounting.

Grab a pen, a coffee, and leave your buzzwords at the door - they won't help you here.

Let's build leaders who know how to lead people, drive profit, and actually get stuff done.

And let's have a few laughs along the way, because if you can't laugh at leadership, you'll cry... and nobody wants a tear-stained strategy document.

You've picked up a book called *Don't Lead Like a Jerk* because, deep down, you know too many workplaces still reward exactly that. Before we can fix it, we need to see how we got here. Chapter 1 is the uncomfortable mirror: why so many smart, well-intentioned people slide into bad-boss territory and why the old rulebook set them up to fail.

CHAPTER 1

WHY LEADERSHIP IS BROKEN (AND WHAT WE'VE BEEN GETTING WRONG)

We've all worked for one. The boss who could sniff out a typo in a 40-page report but couldn't remember your name. The boss who hovered over your shoulder to "help" until you were ready to hurl the mouse at the wall. The boss who avoided every hard conversation until it became a full-blown crisis. The boss who thought motivational leadership meant adding another KPI column to the spreadsheet.

None of them were cartoon villains. Most were good people who wanted to do well - they just ended up leading like jerks.

Here's the thing: almost no one sets out to be that boss. What usually happens is a good performer gets promoted, handed a team, and given zero guidance on how to lead humans.

They fall back on the habits they know - micro-managing, hiding behind numbers, or avoiding conflict - and slowly become the kind of boss they once complained about over Friday drinks. And the truly terrible thing? We are training the next generation of bosses to do the exact same thing when their turn comes around - unless we do something about it.

That's the real story of modern leadership: it's not a few bad apples, it's a system that keeps throwing people into the deep end and hoping they'll swim - then acting shocked when so very many don't.

This chapter looks at how we got here - why so many capable, well-intentioned leaders turn into the bosses we swear we'll never be - and why the old rulebook has to go if we're going to lead people, drive profit, and actually get stuff done.

It's Not Them. It's the System.

If you think the leadership crisis is just a few bad personalities, you're being generous.

Most leaders don't set out to be jerks; they're usually set up to fail by a system that promotes technical stars into people-leadership with no playbook, structure or guidance.

We take a great salesperson, a brilliant engineer, or the most reliable foreman and say:

"You're good at your job - congratulations, you're in charge of people now."

That's it.

No lessons on how to coach adults. No tips on having a tough conversation without crushing morale. Just a laptop, KPIs and a well-meaning "Good luck." Then we're surprised when things go sideways.

The Promotion Trap

Here's how it usually plays out:

Step 1: Someone's brilliant at the technical work.

They're a star engineer, a standout doctor, a designer who can spot the flaw in a sketch from ten metres away, a coder who eats bugs for breakfast (computer joke - sorry), or the manager who knows every system inside out. They're the **quintessential high performer**.

Step 2: We "reward" them with a leadership role.

The logic goes: if they're that good at the work, surely they can get a whole team to be just like them. Perfect - what could go wrong?

Step 3: They assume leadership means telling instead of guiding.

Overnight they go from team-mate to boss and suddenly can't understand why people don't just do what they say. They don't yet know how to coach, influence or hold people accountable, especially when, yesterday, those people were their peers.

Step 4: The team disengages.

The energy drops, eye-rolls increase, and before long the best people quietly start plotting their exit.

It's like promoting your best pastry chef to run the whole restaurant, then wondering why both the soufflés and the staffing collapse.

None of these new leaders set out to be 'that jerk boss' - but the system almost guarantees it.

A Foreman Named Dave

A construction client of ours once promoted their best site foreman - let's call him Dave - to General Site Manager. On-site, Dave was a legend: first to arrive, last to leave, could rally a crew like no one else.

As a manager of managers? Not so much.

He spent the first three months glued to spreadsheets and barely visited the sites.

The crews started calling him "The Invisible Man."

He wasn't lazy or arrogant. He simply didn't know how to lead people he couldn't see every day.

No one had ever shown him.

He also carried around a picture in his head of what "management" was supposed to look like - finally being out of the weather, an office with a door, a bit of privacy and comfort which had been so elusive through hot summers and icy, wet winters. He did not understand the impact of not being present on the ground. He did not yet know what his team now needed of him now that his role had changed.

The Cost of Getting It Wrong

When leadership goes wrong, the fallout shows up everywhere - in the balance sheet, the hallways, the Monday morning moods.

The Destructive Manager

He arrived with a glittering CV and a reputation for "getting results." In his first fortnight he also got two senior colleagues offside, sneered at a long-standing supplier in front of their team, and told a client they'd been "spoilt" by the previous account manager. We'll call him Patrick.

Patrick's style was simple: divide, diminish, dominate. He loved a crisis he could "own," so he quietly fed a few. Projects were pulled forward without warning, then announced in meetings with a flourish and a deadline. When people asked how to resource the new priorities, he'd shrug. "That's why you're here." Staff started skipping him and solving problems informally. He called it insubordination. We called it survival.

The board hesitated. "He's tough but talented," someone said. "Let's give it a quarter." You can guess what happened next. The "tough but talented" leader bled clients. The partner who'd been publicly belittled moved their business within a month. Two high performers asked for internal transfers. Complaints rose. HR kept a folder. Everyone hoped it would blow over.

Then a blow-up forced the issue: Patrick's public dressing-down of a project lead during a client demo. The client - a polite, loyal, conflict-avoidant type - closed their laptop, said, "We'll be in touch," and never came back. That was the invoice the board finally read.

When the termination was announced, people cried. Not because they were cruel, but because they'd been holding their breath for months and someone had finally opened a window. Quietly, we ran listening sessions. You know what we heard? "We didn't need a hero. We needed a grown-up."

Here's the DLPA x-ray: Patrick was all showy Proficiency and "results" theatre, zero People, and a totally warped view of Profit (he confused drama with value). The fix wasn't another charismatic leader. It was trust, role clarity, predictable decision paths - and the humility to treat clients and colleagues like adults.

Within two quarters, the team stabilised. A "no surprises" rule for feedback was introduced. One simple weekly review kept priorities from yo-yoing. Senior leaders started modelling micro-apologies. The culture didn't become perfect; it became safe. That's enough for performance to return.

The cost of getting it wrong can be extreme, but also nuanced and hard to spot at first. Here's what it looks like on the ground:

- Turnover spikes.

People don't leave companies; they leave jerks. Every departure means recruitment fees, training new staff, lost momentum, often equal to 6–9 months of that person's salary gone before you've even hired their replacement.

- Productivity dives.

A disengaged team doesn't innovate; they do the bare minimum to stay out of trouble. You see it in missed deadlines, sloppy quality, or the mysterious two-week delay no one can quite explain.

- Culture rots.

The best people leave first, while others stick around but withdraw and disengage - and the office grapevine starts working harder than the actual team. Suddenly the behaviours you never wanted to see start taking root.

- Customers notice.

Service levels slip, complaints rise, reputation suffers - which eventually shows up in revenue. Pipeline slows and you have to fight even harder for every sale. Your staff feel the squeeze even more.

- Stress spreads upward.

Leaders under pressure tend to push it down the line - often unintentionally. HR gets busy with "interventions," Finance gets busy explaining losses, and the CEO gets busy explaining to the board. The Board wonders what went wrong. The shareholders start to panic.

I once worked with a mid-sized services firm that ignored a toxic team leader for too long.

By the time they acted, three of their top five performers in that unit had quit, customer complaints had doubled, and the cost of turn-over and lost work had topped half a million dollars - all traced back to one under-supported leader.

Gallup's research shows that managers influence roughly 70% of the swings in their team's engagement levels. In other words, the quality of the relationship between a team and its direct manager is often the single biggest factor that decides whether people show up motivated or just show up.

And the cost of getting it wrong is jaw-dropping. In its 2022 State of the Global Workplace report, Gallup estimated that low engagement drains about US $7.8 trillion from the global economy every year - roughly 11% of global GDP. That's the combined drag of missed deadlines, customer churn, absenteeism, presenteeism (people at work but mentally checked-out), and turnover.

Think of it this way: every unmotivated employee is like paying for a full-time salary and getting part-time effort in return - multiplied by millions of people, every day. You don't need the decimal points to know it hurts.

But every point of cost leakage is an opportunity - a chance to plug the gap, win back productivity, and rebuild engagement.

Leadership isn't a "soft" skill. Done well, it's a competitive advantage. Done badly, it's a slow leak in every profit-and-loss statement.

The Myth of the "Born Leader"

Another trap is believing leaders are born, not made.

We've all met someone with natural charisma - but charisma alone rarely survives the first tough quarter.

I once coached a finance director - let's call her Maya - who had an MBA, a brilliant mind for numbers and the confidence of a TED-Talker. A deep understanding of strategy, and absolute clarity about execution.

What she didn't have was patience. Patience for explaining all of those things to others, or for allowing discussion when she was already certain she had the right answer.

Her meetings were 20-minute monologues, usually followed by either stunned silence or polite disengagement.

When we worked on listening skills and feedback conversations, her team's performance jumped. Turns out the missing ingredient wasn't strategy - it was simply connection.

Leadership is a skillset. And with the right structure and deliberate practice, skills can be learned.

How We Got Here

Traditional management models were designed for factory floors - predictable tasks, top-down control, workers assumed to have little autonomy or ambition beyond "do the job and collect the pay." That approach worked well enough when the biggest challenge was keeping everyone tightening the same bolt the same way.

(Though let's be honest, the bit about workers not wanting more than a wage was probably never true.)

Today's workplaces are the opposite: hybrid teams, constant disruption, knowledge work, competing priorities - always being asked to do more with less. For organisations to survive, people now need agency to make quick decisions, not permission slips for every move.

And culturally, the role of work in our lives has shifted. I look at my friends' kids who are now young adults and see a generation that wants no part of their parents' 80-hour weeks.

They want fulfilling work that pays enough to live, but they also want a rich life outside of it - connection to community, meaningful experiences, balance.

We're trying to run a modern tech office with a playbook written for steam engines.

The Three D's of Imbalanced Leadership

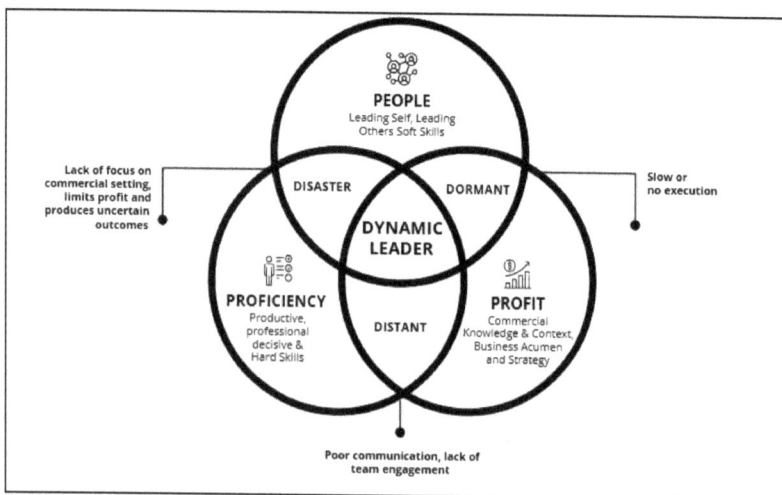

On the DLPA Dynamic Leader model, strong leadership sits at the centre where People, Proficiency and Profit all overlap. If one pillar

is missing, leaders tip into one of the Three D's.

Dormant Leaders – High People & Profit, Low Proficiency

Dormant leaders often understand people and see the bigger commercial picture - they can talk vision and even inspire trust. What's missing is the ability to execute consistently.

They avoid decisions, hope problems will go away, and live by "no news is good news."

You'll recognise them as the manager who hasn't done a performance review in years because "everyone seems fine," or the one who nods along in meetings but never follows through.

They're good at relationships and have commercial instincts, but without the discipline and systems of Proficiency, progress stalls.

Distant Leaders – High Profit & Proficiency, Low People

Distant leaders know their spreadsheets, processes and KPIs inside-out and usually have a solid grasp of how the business makes money. What they miss is the human engine that makes all of that work.

I once met a GM who could recite every financial metric in the company but couldn't name the new team lead sitting two doors down. These leaders tend to bury themselves in reporting, dashboards and inboxes while overlooking how teams actually work together and stay engaged in the mission.

Great at Profit and Proficiency, low on People - and it shows in morale, trust and turnover.

Disaster Leaders – High People & Proficiency, Low Profit

Disaster leaders can be charismatic and inspiring. They rally the team and are often technically strong - great at getting activity underway and keeping people energised. But because they lack commercial and strategic focus, they chase shiny projects, jump from fire drill to fire drill, and mistake busy-ness for progress.

They can tell a strong story about why people should follow them - and they do - but without a sound Profit/strategy pillar, they can lead that motivated team straight off a cliff.

Most leaders don't choose to be a Dormant, Distant or Disaster type - they slide into it when one pillar is neglected. Spotting which pillar is missing is the first step toward getting back to the centre: the Dynamic Leader zone.

A Tale of Two Team Leads

A professional-services client had two rising stars promoted to team lead within months of each other.

Ellie* was warm, good at checking in with her people, but allergic to tough conversations.

Her team loved her... right up until deadlines slipped and clients complained. Then they started worrying they were going to miss out on promotions because their leader wasn't strong enough.

Tom* was decisive, fantastic at process, but had the empathy of a wet sponge in winter.

He got results, but his staff turnover was higher than the city's rent prices. His team delivered results for short bursts, but then they burned out and left. Or worse, burned out and stayed - only to poison the ecosystem further. Eventually the overall performance started to slip as well.

Neither was "bad" - they were simply leaning on one pillar of leadership and ignoring the other two. Both turned things around after focusing on developing more balanced ability across the three pillars - People, Proficiency and Profit - and giving those skills oxygen, and flexing those muscles every single day.

The DLPA Dynamic Leader Lens

That's the core of this book: the DLPA Dynamic Leader model - a simple, memorable way to lead.

People – lead humans, not just job titles. Build trust, culture, resilience. Lead yourself, lead others and lead the organisation.

Proficiency – set clear expectations, solve problems, get the work done. Understand the technical nature of the work those you lead do, and support them to be more productive and effective.

Profit – understand how the business wins, so the team's effort actually matters. Have strong business acumen, strategic understanding and appreciation of context.

Miss one leg of that stool, and down it goes.

What This Chapter Sets Up

Before we build Dynamic Leaders, we need to be honest about why the old rulebook isn't working anymore. Consider this chapter the mirror: uncomfortable but necessary.

Reflection Corner

Think of the best leader you ever worked for.

- What did they do that made you feel motivated?

Now think of the worst.

- Which behaviours made them hard to follow?
- Where do you recognise shades of either in yourself?

Write it down. You'll use it later.

Closing Beat

Leadership isn't broken because leaders are bad people, or because leaders don't care. It's broken because we've been using an outdated playbook that belongs to a different century in a modern game. The good news? Rulebooks can and should be rewritten.

In the next chapter, we'll explore the Dynamic Leader framework - the antidote to the Three D's - and start building a leadership style that works for real people, in the real world. Knowing what's broken is only half the job. Now we need a new playbook. Chapter 2 introduces the DLPA Dynamic Leader model: the framework that keeps leaders balanced across People, Proficiency and Profit so we don't drift back into jerk mode when we are under pressure.

THE DYNAMIC LEADER FRAMEWORK: PEOPLE, PROFICIENCY AND PROFIT

The Day the Team Broke

On paper, the company was cruising. A construction-services outfit with a reputation for being fast, lean and profitable. In reality, the wheels were starting to wobble.

It began quietly: two engineers on stress leave, a customer escalation that took weeks to resolve, an HR complaint about "unreasonable workload expectations."

The warning lights were blinking, but leadership didn't notice - or pretended not to.

Monday, 8:15 a.m. – The Crisis Call

The first real crack showed up in a Monday stand-up that felt more like a hostage negotiation.

Cameras off, voices flat, every update a mix of apology and defensiveness. Deadlines had slipped - again.

"People just need to step up," said Mark*, the newly-minted project director.

He'd been promoted for being brilliant at scoping technical solutions, not for calming fractious humans. Mark genuinely believed he was motivating the team; in reality he was pouring petrol on their anxiety.

One of the senior drafters, Priya*, spoke up:

"I've been across three projects for months. I don't know which one's top priority anymore. I can't keep doing late nights just to watch priorities change on Friday, and have to re-do all my work again."

No one responded. Mark cleared his throat, said "We'll take that offline," and moved to the next person. The tension in the Zoom chat could have powered the site compounds.

The Week Unravels

By Wednesday, the safety officer lodged a near-miss incident report - a rushed overnight change that hadn't been communicated to the field crew.

By Thursday, a junior estimator resigned by email citing "burnout."

By Friday, a client escalated to the COO about slipping delivery milestones and issued a Show Cause letter.

HR's weekend inbox included two complaints: one about bullying tone in emails, another about "being set up to fail" due to shifting goals and a feeling that information was being withheld.

The COO's Monday dashboard showed sick-leave spiking 18% above baseline.

Beneath the Surface – Hazards Everywhere

If you looked closely, the same story kept repeating:

- High job demands – excessive workload, long hours, weekend "urgent" calls.
- Low role clarity – shifting priorities, no one sure who owned which decisions.
- Poor support – new hybrid policy meant leaders rarely checked in face-to-face.
- Poor change management – plans changed every week with no explanation.
- Perceived unfairness – some staff repeatedly pulled in to 'save' late projects.

None of this appeared in the glossy board pack.

These pressures aren't new.

They've always been part of the real world of work; we simply used to accept them as "just how it is." Today we understand far better - and can prove with data - that they harm people's mental health, drive turnover, and drag down performance.

Safety regulators now include these factors under the banner of psychosocial hazards, but the science behind them has been in the organisational-psychology literature for decades.

We just finally have the vocabulary - and, increasingly, the legal duty - to call them what they are.

Friday, 4:45 p.m. – The Breaking Point

Late Friday, a foreman named Lee* - normally one of the calmest people in the room - walked into Mark's office and said,

"If we don't slow down, someone's going to get hurt out there. This isn't just stress anymore. People aren't being soft or whingey - the work just can't be done this way."

That was the moment the team effectively broke: when the frontline lost faith that leadership had their backs. Mark looked blindsided. He wasn't a bad guy; quite the opposite, he wanted to support the team and really believed they did great work. He genuinely hadn't realised how fragile the team had become.

He'd been so busy juggling forecasts and budgets that he stopped noticing the people doing the work, and had sailed past all the red flags.

Monday Debrief

The COO called an emergency leadership meeting. They didn't talk about profits first.

They talked about psychological safety notices, a potential workers compensation claim for a stress-related injury, and the risk of losing two more senior staff.

For the first time, the executive team saw the connection: the very leadership behaviours they thought were "pushing for results" were the same behaviours driving errors, turnover and rising costs.

What Really Broke

It wasn't just a tough week. It was a slow erosion of three critical things:

- People – trust, inclusion, genuine two-way conversation.
- Proficiency – clear expectations, role clarity, disciplined execution.
- Profit focus – not just chasing revenue but prioritising the right work at the right pace.

The team had two of these some of the time, never all three at once. Whenever one leg of the stool went missing, stress filled the gap.

The Leadership Lesson

This story isn't unusual. Most teams that "break" don't do so overnight - it happens drip by drip: skipped conversations, unmade decisions, shifting goals, leaders juggling so many fires they forget to lead.

Good leadership isn't just about being nice or hitting the target. It's about protecting people from foreseeable harm and getting the right work done in the right way. Done well, it's the strongest psychosocial hazard control a business has.

That's what this chapter is about - how Dynamic Leaders balance People, Proficiency and Profit to build teams that not only deliver but stay healthy doing it.

Good Leadership Is a Risk-Control Strategy

When people talk about "psychosocial hazards" it can sound like new HR jargon or soft fluffy stuff, but the truth is that these conditions have always been there. For as long as humans have worked, we've been affected by how we're led, how our work is organised, how change is handled, and whether we feel safe to speak up.

Long before regulators coined the term, leaders who set clear expectations, treated people fairly, and supported them through change were protecting their people's mental health - they just didn't necessarily call it that.

Leadership Choices Create or Control the Risks

Most of the common hazards show up when one of the three pillars - People, Proficiency, Profit - is neglected:

- Poor workload design or constant last-minute crises - high job demands, fatigue, burnout.

- Lack of clarity on roles, priorities, or authority - conflict, mistakes, stress.
- Leaders who disappear behind emails or dashboards - low support, low trust, higher turnover.
- Change launched without context or follow-through - uncertainty, frustration, disengagement.
- Targets pushed without balancing resources - moral injury, cynicism, long-term health costs.

None of these are "soft" issues. They have measurable impacts on error rates, absenteeism, compensation claims, turnover and revenue leakage.

The Leadership Shield

The right leadership behaviours act like a shield:

- People pillar - trust, fairness, inclusion, respect, psychological safety.
- Proficiency pillar - role clarity, competence, workflow discipline, predictable pace of work.
- Profit pillar - realistic prioritisation, transparency about trade-offs, stable strategy.

When leaders keep these three in balance, they're not just making the workplace nicer - they're reducing foreseeable harm, improving resilience and lifting performance.

Put simply: Dynamic Leaders don't wait for regulators to tell them to manage psychosocial risks. They already do it, because it's part of leading well.

Why It Matters Now

Hybrid work, talent shortages and relentless cost-pressure have made these factors harder to ignore:

- More autonomy means greater need for clarity and communication.

- Faster change cycles mean more risk of overload and confusion.

- Tighter margins mean every hour of disengagement or turnover has a visible cost.

Leaders who still think their job is to "stay out of HR stuff and focus on results" are missing the point: the way you lead is the biggest controllable factor in both wellbeing *and* results.

In the next pages we'll break down the three pillars of the DLPA Dynamic Leader Framework - People, Proficiency, Profit - and show, with stories and data, how each one protects your people and powers your business.

The DLPA Dynamic Leader Framework isn't a fad or just another slide deck. It's the same structure we use when we're asked to run leadership workshops, coach executives or redesign whole people-projects and change programs.

Sometimes clients call because they want a single workshop. More often, the workshop is just the doorway into something deeper: fixing the habits and systems that are quietly burning people out, stalling change and leaking profit.

Whenever we diagnose what's really happening underneath the complaints or pain points - "communication issues," "low engagement," "too much change fatigue" - it nearly always traces back to an imbalance in one of the three DLPA pillars: People, Proficiency or Profit.

Strengthen all three, and leaders stop firefighting, employees feel supported, psychosocial risks drop, change sticks, and the organisation finally does what the subtitle of this book promises:

lead people, drive profit, and actually get stuff done - without leading like a jerk.

Pillar 1: PEOPLE – Lead Humans First

What Goes Wrong

Most "jerk" stories we hear in leadership coaching start here. A leader forgets that the "resources" they're managing are, inconveniently, people with needs, limits, ambitions, thoughts, feelings and personal lives.

Typical warning signs we see during people-projects:
- Leaders skip one-on-ones because "my door's always open" (translation: good luck catching me between back-to-back meetings).
- High performers are rewarded with... more work and no recognition.
- Introverts are overlooked because they don't shout about achievements.

- Feedback is delayed until the annual review - when it's either too late or too vague to matter.

All of these trigger well-researched psychosocial hazards: low support, lack of recognition, perceived unfairness, interpersonal conflict. They show up as disengagement, quiet resentment and eventually turnover.

A Story: The Over-It Engineer

In one infrastructure client, we met Hannah*, a high-performing civil engineer. She'd been on three consecutive "priority" projects for 18 months, had worked most weekends, and was the go-to problem-solver. Her manager thought he was recognising her by "trusting her with the critical jobs." He thought she was wonderful and wanted to see how she could take on more exciting projects.

Hannah saw it as being punished for competence.

Eventually Hannah was at breaking point and ended up lodging a workers compensation claim for a psychological injury. The subsequent investigation highlighted unsustainable workload and lack of support as the main contributory factors for the injury.

The fix wasn't a mindfulness app; it was coaching her leader to plan resources properly, redistribute load, and have weekly check-ins that included 'thank-you, here's what's coming next.' Sadly for Hannah, this insight came too late.

A leader who thinks "treat everyone the same" is being fair often ends up treating everyone equally badly.

Humans will usually forgive a leader who makes an honest mistake. They rarely forgive a leader who leaves them unseen, unheard, or treated as interchangeable widgets in a de-humanised system. Trust erosion in the People pillar leaks straight into:

- lower discretionary effort,
- resistance to change,
- higher turnover,
- more HR complaints.

People-Pillar Strength Looks Like:

- Role clarity + respect + timely, specific feedback.
- Leaders who spot early fatigue and adjust workload before it breaks people.
- Inclusion in change conversations before the change hits.
- Recognition that's meaningful, not just a pizza voucher.

Dynamic Leaders build these habits so they can lead humans, not just job titles - and in doing so, head off a big chunk of psychosocial risk.

Pillar 2: PROFICIENCY – Get Stuff Done Without the Drama

If the People pillar is how we treat each other, Proficiency is how we organise the work.

Neglect this and even the nicest leader starts to look like a jerk.

Where We See Trouble

Common in change-management projects we run:

- Priorities change every Monday; nobody knows what's dropped.
- Processes so over-engineered that no one follows them.
- Or the opposite - zero process, constant "urgent" work.
- New software rolled out with training that's basically a PDF and good luck.
- Leaders dodge making decisions, so bottlenecks pile up.

These are not character flaws; they're structural gaps that create role conflict, chronic job demands, perceived lack of control - which are all recognised psychosocial hazards.

Story: The Email Factory

A professional-services client once prided itself on "agility." In practice that meant every client manager could promise anything to any customer at any time - regardless of what could actually be delivered. Delivery teams lived in their inboxes, waiting for the next fire to break out.

We mapped the work and found 46 % of effort was re-work or urgent last-minute reshuffling.

Staff reported high stress and zero confidence in meeting deadlines. This led to zero engagement in actually attempting to achieve deadlines. Clients were unhappy, because they had been promised the impossible, and were disappointed to discover it really was too good to be true.

By introducing:

- weekly prioritisation huddles,
- clear work-in-progress limits,
- a simple RACI chart for who could promise what, when and for what benefit,

...error rates fell 30 % and sick-leave dropped in one quarter.

The leader didn't become "nicer" - they became more proficient, which lowered stress.

A team without clear roles is like herding cats...on rollerskates.

People don't burn out from hard work; they burn out from pointless, chaotic, constantly-shifting work. That's why Proficiency isn't bureaucracy - it's stress-prevention infrastructure.

Proficiency-Pillar Strength Looks Like:

- Clear goals and boundaries for each role.
- Realistic workload pacing - no heroics as standard.
- Decisions made by the right person at the right level.
- Change rolled out with a comms plan that's more than 47 unread emails.

Dynamic Leaders keep Proficiency strong to protect both output and people from chaos-induced stress.

Pillar 3: PROFIT – Direction, Priorities and the 'Why'

Many leaders still feel awkward talking openly about money, as if keeping commercial goals secret makes them noble or more valuable in some way. Ironically, that silence often turns them into the jerk boss: "Run harder, I can't tell you why, just trust me."

When teams understand how their work connects to profit and purpose:

- they prioritise better,
- they make smarter trade-offs,
- they show more resilience during change because they understand the "why".

A weak Profit pillar breeds hazards of its own:

- endless pivots = uncertainty, wasted effort;
- unrealistic revenue pushes = moral injury, cynicism, burnout;
- budget secrecy = rumours, fear, disengagement.

Story: The Vanishing Target

An IT company we worked with shifted strategy four times in 12 months without ever explaining the commercial drivers to staff. Teams chased each new target hard, only to watch it vanish behind the next "pivot." Strategy started to feel like a fad instead of a driving force or true North. Activity started to wane.

By the third swing, engagement scores dived and high performers stopped volunteering for innovation sprints.

When we coached the executive team to share the economic context and stop chasing low-value pet projects and instead embedding strategy through multiple iterative cycles, employees started suggesting better cost-saving ideas than leadership had identified.

Profit transparency rebuilt trust and morale.

For clarity, this does not mean that you need to share commercial secrets with all and sundry. The strategy must be broken down into meaningful chunks so that you can clearly express to each and every member of your team how they add value to the organisation every day. Transparency does not mean show everything - it simply means don't hide information individuals need to know to have the context of how their work matters.

Strategy shouldn't feel like chasing a Pokémon - just when you think you've got it, it disappears behind another bush. Strategy must be the beating heart of an organisation, and the compass which guides every action. And it must exist for long enough for people to really be connected to it.

Profit-Pillar Strength Looks Like

- Transparent goals and trade-offs.
- Leaders willing to say "no" to low-value work.
- Commercially-savvy teams who link daily tasks to meaningful outcomes, and understand what makes an organisation tick.

Dynamic Leaders keep Profit visible and honest - so their teams can stop running in circles and get the right stuff done.

Most of the behaviours that make a boss feel like a jerk - e.g. snapping at staff, micromanaging, pushing late-night demands - are symptoms of a weak pillar. Strengthen all three pillars and you not only hit the numbers, you reduce psychosocial risk, lower turnover and make change stick. And you create great places to work.

That's what we do in our DLPA projects: diagnose which pillar is out of balance, build the leader's skill there, and integrate the fix into change-management plans so it sticks long after the workshop's over.

Dynamic Leaders vs Hazards

The best way to see why the three pillars matter is to eavesdrop on two teams who faced the same challenge - same company, same software, same deadline - but two very different leaders.

The Great Platform Migration

A mid-sized professional-services firm had just merged with a competitor. Every client account had to be migrated onto a single new platform within six months without losing a single customer or missing billing. What could possibly go wrong??

Enter Team A and Team B.

Same size, same skills, same budget. The only real difference was the person steering the ship and the culture they were used to operating in.

Team A – Spreadsheet at the Helm

Amir*, the Team A leader, was brilliant with the technical side. Unfortunately, he thought "leadership" meant a heroic relationship with Excel. For the first fortnight he barely looked up from the migration tracker. Priorities changed almost daily; no one knew which client was really first in line. When workloads spiked, his answer was the classic: "We'll just have to dig deeper, folks."

One Friday he emailed at 10 p.m. to say a major deadline had moved forward - because apparently sleep is optional and weekends don't exist. Two senior analysts quietly started applying for transfers and new positions. Sick-leave shot up. They hit the final deadline, but only by pulling weekend shifts that blew out overtime and goodwill. Quality control found enough errors to wipe out any profit gain, and two valuable customers left after the first month of hiccups.

Hazards unleashed: high demands, low clarity, low support, a grand sense of unfairness.

Team B – The Balanced Act

Leila*, leading Team B, was no saint and not a natural cheerleader - but she worked deliberately across all three DLPA pillars.

Profit first (context, not secrecy). She kicked off with a team huddle to explain why the migration mattered commercially and what was at stake if they got it wrong. When people see the scoreboard, they play smarter.

Proficiency next (how we'll get it done). Leila mapped out roles, owners and decision points before the first deadline hit. Weekly check-ins were short and mandatory: "Are we on track, do you have what you need, what's blocking you?"

People always (don't break the humans). She set up a five-minute Friday "pulse-check" - traffic-light style - to catch stress or risk areas early. She recognised extra effort publicly in the team chat and negotiated one extra contractor for the two peak weeks instead of pretending caffeine was a workload plan.

Results:

- Deadlines met with fewer weekend hours.
- Zero turnover.
- Quality scores much higher than Team A.
- Engagement survey up 11 points in six months.

Hazards reduced: clearer roles, moderated demands, higher perceived fairness and support.

The Punchline

Both leaders were technically competent. But Amir's imbalance - strong on Proficiency and Profit, weak on People - cranked up stress and risk until it bit him in the P&L.

Leila's balance controlled the risk at the source and proved you can drive profit and keep your team intact.

A Dynamic Leader isn't softer; they're just smarter about where to push and where to protect.

They apply pressure to the work, not to the people.

Dynamic Leaders hold all three so the team can get the right stuff done without breaking themselves in the process.

Leadership that ignores a pillar is like rowing a boat with one oar - you go in circles and eventually hit something.

Three Things the Dynamic Leader Did Differently

- Shared the Profit context up-front - people knew the "why" behind the push.
- Built Proficiency systems before the workload peaked - so work flowed instead of jammed.
- Kept the People practices visible - check-ins, recognition, sane boundaries.

That's not fluff. That's how you cut stress, hold talent, protect culture and still deliver.

Good leadership isn't about being everyone's best friend or running pizza Fridays.

It's about removing avoidable friction and risk so the humans can do their best work.

When you do that, engagement goes up and profit follows - the whole point of this book's subtitle:

lead people, drive profit, and actually get stuff done.

Thriving People, Thriving Organisations

We've seen the hazards. Now here's the upside: when leaders get the three pillars right, the payoff is massive - for the humans and for the numbers.

The Jerk Tax Is Real

Every time a leader behaves like a jerk - snapping at staff, shifting priorities on Friday afternoon, dodging tough conversations - the business pays what we call the Jerk Tax:

- Higher turnover - recruitment, onboarding and lost productivity.
- Burnout - more sick-leave and comp claims.
- Poor change adoption - wasted project spend.
- Disengaged staff - customers notice, revenue suffers.

Gallup has been telling us for decades that engaged teams are 21 % more profitable and 17 % more productive than disengaged ones.

In its 2022 State of the Global Workplace report, it estimated low engagement costs the global economy US $7.8 trillion a year - around 11 % of global GDP. This is a staggering amount which is near impossible to actually get your head around.

Translation: the Jerk Tax is one of the world's largest unbudgeted expenses.

Profit Loves Engagement

When leaders balance People + Proficiency + Profit, three good things happen at once:

- Turnover drops – replacing a mid-level employee costs roughly 6–9 months of their salary in lost productivity and hiring expense.
- Change sticks – projects with excellent change management

are 6× more likely to meet or beat their objectives (Prosci research).

- Wellbeing lifts – employees who feel supported are 3× more likely to stay with the organisation and report higher energy at work.

That combination compounds: less churn, fewer delays, steadier revenue, lower recruitment spend — and fewer awkward board conversations.

Story: The CFO's Surprise Windfall

One of our clients - a national logistics business - didn't come to us asking for culture work; they came asking why their overtime bill was exploding. It turned out the overtime was a symptom: staff turnover in the distribution centres had hit nearly 38 % a year because shift supervisors were stuck in Dormant-leader mode (great with people, hopeless with process).

We worked with them on Proficiency - better rostering, clear job expectations, regular one-on-ones - and a bit of Profit context so everyone knew why the changes mattered.

Results after six months:

- overtime spend down 26 %,
- turnover halved,
- injury claims fell by a third.

The CFO called it "the cheapest productivity program we ever ran."

Wellbeing Isn't HR Fluff - It's Risk Management

Wellbeing doesn't need to be fluff (although let's be honest, sometimes it is). When implemented strategically, and with focus, it can fundamentally shift an organisation's performance. Stronger leadership in the People pillar also acts as a psychosocial-hazard control:

- clearer roles reduce role-conflict stress,
- visible support reduces perceived unfairness,
- steadier workloads reduce burnout risk.

That's not a "soft" return - it's fewer stress-leave claims, fewer grievances, better safety stats and steadier customer delivery.

We often tell executives: "You can spend on better leadership now, or you can keep paying the Jerk Tax later - plus interest."

The Triple Win

The DLPA framework is built for a triple win:

- People thrive - less churn, better ideas, fewer complaints.
- Proficiency hums - less chaos, less re-work, fewer late-night 'surprises'.
- Profit grows - steadier margins, fewer cost-leaks, better customer retention.

This is the sweet spot promised on the cover: lead people, drive profit, and actually get stuff done.

In the next (and final) part of this chapter we'll give you a Reflection Corner - a quick self-scan of your own leadership habits - so you can see where you're strong and where you might be quietly paying the Jerk Tax.

Reflection Corner

Before we charge ahead to Chapter 3, take five minutes for a reality-check.

You can't build new habits on top of old blind spots.

Grab a pen (or scribble in the margin - I won't tell or judge) and be brutally honest.

Circle, tick, underline... whatever works.

This isn't graded; it's for you.

Step 1 – Gut-Check on the Three Pillars

For each statement, give yourself a quick score:

1 = Needs work   3 = It's OK   5 = Nailed it

People – Lead Humans First

- I have regular, purposeful one-on-ones with each direct report.
- I give timely, specific feedback - not just at annual review time.
- My team would say I notice when the load's too heavy and do something about it.
- When change is coming, I explain the why before the rumour mill does.

- I treat people fairly - not identically, but fairly.

Proficiency – Get Stuff Done Without the Drama

- Everyone on my team knows what success looks like in their role this quarter.

- We plan the work so "urgent" is the exception, not the weekly theme.

- We fix bottlenecks and decision delays fast.

- New tools or processes come with proper comms and training, not just a link.

- We keep our team's priorities short enough that everyone can name the top three without peeking at a slide deck

Profit – Direction, Priorities and the 'Why'

- I can explain in one sentence how our team contributes to revenue, savings or impact.

- I say no to low-value work often enough to protect focus.

- I share the scoreboard (results, wins, lessons) openly with the team.

- My team understands which customers / projects matter most right now.

- Strategy feels stable enough that people believe next month's priorities will still matter next month.

Step 2 – Spot Your Tilt

Look at your scores.

Highest pillar = your natural comfort zone.

Lowest pillar = where you're most likely to accidentally lead like a jerk.

That low pillar is usually where the psychosocial hazards creep in - the source of your Jerk Tax.

Step 3 – Micro-Commitments

Write down one small thing you'll do in the next 7 days to shore up that weakest pillar.

(Examples: book a 20-min check-in with each team member, kill one zombie project, explain the why behind the next change.)

You don't need to be perfect. You just need to be one jerk-habit less this week than you were last week.

Looking Ahead

This reflection is your personal baseline. In the next chapter we'll get into the practical tools and habits that turn those three pillars into muscle-memory - so you can lead people, drive profit, and actually get stuff done without drifting back into jerk-mode.

Of the three pillars, the first - People - is the one leaders most often think they're good at...and usually really aren't. We see many leaders confused by tanking engagement scores and confronting exit interviews when they thought they were acing it. In Chapter 3 we will unpack what it really takes to lead humans in a way that builds trust instead of drama.

CHAPTER 3

HOW TO LEAD PEOPLE (AND NOT LOSE YOUR MIND DOING IT)

"Monday Morning with Marcus" Monday morning. Marcus*, a newly minted team leader, had been up half the night perfecting his pep talk. He strode into the meeting room armed with a PowerPoint, a quote from Mandela, and the determination to be "inspirational."

His team? They were armed with coffee, deadlines and the hope of escaping in under 15 minutes with no more than 3 eye rolls.

Marcus clicked to slide one: "Together We Soar!" There was a suitably cliche stock image of an eagle. By slide three, someone coughed loud enough to sound like a laugh. By slide six, half the team were checking emails under the table. By slide eight most of the team were checking emails on top of the table. When he finally reached the crescendo - "We are not just colleagues, we are FAMILY!" - the IT specialist actually snorted into her latte. This freed the group to openly laugh. Marcus felt crushed.

The problem wasn't that Marcus was a bad person or particularly bad leader. It was that he thought leading people meant performing at them. And he was doing a version of what he had seen leaders do. Except he didn't have the experience of the nous to land it.

What his team really needed that Monday was:

- a quick update on which project was top priority,
- clarity on who was covering the late client request,
- and to know that their leader had noticed they were still catching up from last week's fire drill.

They didn't need a TED Talk or a surrogate work family. They needed a leader who listened first, then talked, understood the coalface and was willing to get in the trenches with them.

Leading people isn't about having the perfect speech, being everyone's therapist, or staging a motivational flash mob. It's about making work clearer, fairer and calmer so they can do their best work - and not secretly update their résumés at lunch.

That's why this chapter zooms in on the first pillar of the DLPA model: People.

Because no matter how sharp your strategy or spreadsheet, if you can't lead humans well, the rest is just noise.

Leading Yourself First

If you can't lead yourself, you'll always end up accidentally leading like a jerk. That's not character assassination - it's physics: stress rolls downhill.

Leaders who snap at people, micromanage the oxygen out of the room, or disappear behind their inbox aren't born villains. They're usually just tired, overloaded, under-resourced and reacting instead of leading. Equally, leaders who just don't understand what motivates their team, or want people to act exactly to some stereotype, aren't necessarily bad leaders either - they've just never been shown how to effectively lead people and meet them where they are.

Before you start fixing everyone else, you have to know your own triggers, limits and habits - otherwise you'll keep exporting your stress to the team.

The Mirror Nobody Likes

You can't manage what you won't admit or won't look at.

Ask yourself, honestly:

- What's my default move under pressure: control everything, avoid everything, or over-talk everything? Blow everything up? Conflate and catastrophise every issue that has gone before into this present issue?
- How do I show up in a crisis - calm voice, or caffeine-fuelled auctioneer? Fear-monger, absent leader or paralysed.
- When I'm stressed, do I get sharper and shorter, or quieter

and harder to read?

- What kind of leader do my team see at 4 p.m. on a bad Thursday?

Write it down.

(Yes, really. Don't just nod and move on - that's how bad habits survive.)

Triggers: The Jerk Switch

Every leader has a jerk switch - the things that trip you from reasonable human to eye-rolling tyrant.

Common culprits we see in coaching:

- Unclear expectations from your own boss.
- A calendar packed so tight you need an air-traffic controller.
- Fear of conflict, so you delay tough calls until they're urgent.
- Your phone pinging like a Vegas slot-machine.
- Three nights in a row of four-hour sleep.

Most of those aren't personality flaws; they're signal lights that your personal operating system is overloaded.

My jerk switch is when I think people are disrespectful with my time. It bothers me all the time, but if someone expects me to drop everything for their "urgent" request, or demands I finish a task in an unreasonable timeframe - and I've had a poor sleep or it's already a manic week - I morph into a rampaging dragon-lady.

We all have a jerk switch. Knowing what and where it is is the first step to avoiding flipping it.

Boundaries: Lead Your Calendar or It Will Lead You

One of the most effective psychosocial-hazard controls you'll ever deploy is boundaries - mostly around time. If you can't lead your own calendar, good luck leading humans. Most of us are slaves to our calendars, running from meeting to meeting, and deadline to deadline without ever really stopping to think why. Whose agenda are we following? Who is beating that drum we are dancing to? Every effective leader must protect their time like the most valuable commodity it is. Clear boundaries on time not give you more capacity to lead, it gives your team permission to do the same. In a world addicted to busyness, this is the key life skill we all need.

Practical basics:

- Think in energy, not just hours. Book your hardest conversations for when you're mentally fresher.

- Build white space. If there's no breathing room between meetings, you'll start reacting instead of thinking.

- Protect one predictable switch-off. It could be the gym, school pickup, dog-walk - whatever keeps you human.

- Use 1:1s wisely. Make them sacred; don't keep bumping them for "urgent" tasks. But equally, make them count.

A Quick Self-Scan

Score yourself 1-to-5 on these:

- I know my biggest stress triggers and how they show up in my behaviour.
- I protect at least one non-negotiable daily boundary.
- My team would say my reactions are consistent, even under pressure.
- I block thinking-time on my calendar and defend it like a meeting with the board.
- I've apologised at least once for losing it or not being my best self in crisis - and meant it.

Anything under 3 is a flag that your self-leadership needs attention before you pile on new leadership hacks.

The Pay-off

Leaders who manage their own stress show up clearer, calmer and less reactive - which is half of leading people well. They make better decisions, have better conversations, and don't export chaos to the team. It's also the fastest way to shrink a big psychosocial hazard: the one called "unpredictable boss."

Trust: The Non-Negotiable Currency

You can have the best strategy, the slickest tech, and KPIs so colourful they look like a Christmas tree. If your team doesn't trust you, none of it sticks. They'll nod in meetings, smile in town-halls, and quietly do their own thing anyway.

Trust is **the** currency of leadership. Without it, every decision costs twice as much energy to land. With it, even tough changes get a fair hearing.

Trust Beats Charisma

A lot of leaders think they need to be charismatic to win hearts. Not so. Charisma is great at a launch party or even a job interview; it won't carry you through a budget cut. People don't follow charm long term; they follow leaders who are predictable, honest and fair. The quickest way to build trust isn't a stirring speech - it's doing what you said you'd do.

The Problem is You

A media company invited us to help with "a bit of morale trouble." That phrase usually means "everything is on fire, please bring a garden hose." We interviewed widely. People liked the brand and the work. They didn't like feeling invisible, hearing priorities change by rumour, or watching the boss yo-yo between inspirational visionary and sarcastic sniper.

When we sat down with the CEO, I said, "Good news and bad news. The good news: the root cause is clear. The bad news: it's you."

Silence. Then, to his credit, he didn't bark or deflect. He said, "Say more." We showed him what his team had described: cancelling one-on-ones whenever something shinier arrived, sharing half-plans in town halls that triggered a month of anxiety, punishing when people said they didn't know the answer immediately and lashing out when numbers dipped. We also showed him his strengths: sharp instincts, genuine care, a sense of humour that, when not weaponised, lifted the room.

We proposed three experiments. One: re-instate 1:1s and keep them unless the building is literally on fire (even then, do them at the muster point). Two: adopt a "no surprises" rule - if hard news is coming, he would own and explain it early. Three: a micro-apology in public when he snapped. Not a martyr routine; a sentence and a reset.

He did them. The first apology was awkward. He walked back into a meeting five hours after a blow-up and said, "I was frustrated about the numbers and took it out on the room. That's on me. Here's the data and what I'm worried about. Let's talk solutions." People were stunned. Then relieved. Then productive.

Within a quarter, the annualised turnover rate nudged down. Exit interviews mentioned "renewed trust." We also coached him on the "why-for-them" - every change announcement came with context, not just instructions. He still had sharp edges. He learned to sand them fast.

That's the People pillar in the wild. Trust isn't charisma; it's predictable behaviour under pressure. Candour plus care is not a poster - it's how you show up when you're tired and the numbers are red. And sometimes the bravest leadership act is to hear, "The problem is you," and make that sentence untrue next quarter.

Four Building Blocks of Trust

1. Competence – "You know your stuff."

   Your team doesn't expect you to have all the answers, but they do need to believe you understand the work enough to back them up, and understand an issue if they bring it to you.

2. Consistency – "You show up the same way on Monday as you did on Friday."

   Nothing drains trust faster than a leader who's cheerful one day and fire-breathing the next, especially when there is no visibility for why. The data shows that people consistently prefer a known negative outcome to an uncertain one. Inconsistent leaders foster mistrust and stress.

3. Candour – "You tell us the truth, even when it's awkward."

   Leaders who dodge the tough conversations create bigger rumours than the problem itself. I worked with a leader once who was known for his truth telling, and leaning into even the most awkward conversations. He wasn't the most charismatic, he didn't have the deepest commercial acumen, but people trusted that what he was saying was the truth as he knew it, and as such they trusted his advice and his narrative.

4. Care – "You notice we're human."

   Care isn't a cupcake day or a poster on the wall once a year; it's asking how someone's doing and actually listening to the answer. It's understanding that humans are complex, flawed and glorious beings, and meeting them where they are.

Story – The Apology That Changed the Room

A GM I worked with, let's call her Renee* was known for being sharp and results-driven - and for terrifying new starters and sometimes the not so new starters (maybe even me at some points in time). One particularly stressful quarter she snapped at a senior analyst during a meeting. Later that day she walked back into the same meeting room, in front of the same group, and said:

"I was out of line earlier. I was frustrated about the numbers, not at you. I'm sorry."

The whole tone of the team shifted after that. Productivity didn't spike overnight, but morale and openness did - because people saw that she owned her mistake. There was a level of surprise that she had so openly and completely apologised, but also awareness that the apology was genuine and that she had decided she couldn't leave the behaviour out in the ecosystem as acceptable.

That one act built more trust than a dozen cupcake days or picnic days. It also showed the team it was OK to make mistakes, as long as you owned them and built a better path forward.

Psychosocial Safety Link

Low trust fuels some of the nastiest psychosocial hazards:
- perceived unfairness and lack of organisational justice,
- lack of voice in decisions,

- high stress from unclear motives.

It's also the open door to bullying.

Leaders who build trust lower that risk at the source - they create a climate where people feel safe to speak up, ask for help, and admit mistakes before they become disasters.

Trust is like fitness: you can't buy it, you build it - and if you stop working at it, it sags.

Quick Trust Self-Scan

Score 1–5:

- I keep my promises - even the small ones.
- My reactions are consistent; no one wonders which version of me will show up today.
- I tell people the "why" behind tough decisions, not just the headline.
- I listen without rushing to the next meeting.
- If I screw up, I admit it - preferably before someone else announces it.

Anything below 3 is where to focus first.

Trust isn't a side-project; it's the groundwork for every other leadership skill you'll read about in this book.

Communication That Lands

Most leaders think they're better communicators than they actually are. They confuse talking with communicating, and then wonder why everyone's still confused. I worked with a CEO who would often rant about his frustration that everyone around him was such a bad communicator. It was a slightly awkward conversation when I had to point out that I had observed the issue was that people didn't understand his communication, or he was just flat out not communicating critical information. People were dazed, confused and annoyed about being told they hadn't communicated about something they didn't even know existed.

Great communication isn't about how many words you use - it's about how much clarity lands on the other side. It's also not about how well you understood your message. If they didn't hear it, understand it, or believe it, you didn't communicate.

The Buzzword Filter

A quick way to make sure your message doesn't land: load it with corporate buzzwords.

We've all sat through the announcement that "we're embarking on a synergistic transformation journey to optimise cross-functional alignment."

Translation: no one knows what's changing or why. And don't start me on 'pivots'.

Rule: If you wouldn't use the word over dinner with a friend, don't use it in a meeting at work. And if you think someone sounds like a - let's say so-and-so - when they use a word, guess what? So do you.

"Buzzwords don't inspire anyone but consultants. Try nouns and verbs your team already speaks."

Start with the Why, Not the Slide Deck

Most resistance to change isn't because people hate change; it's because they don't understand why it matters. OK, most people hate change. But they hate it a bit less if they understand the why.

Always lead with context before content. If you can't explain why in two sentences, you're not ready to roll it out. And not just why it matters to you. Communication is about having the other party hear and understand your message. Tell them why it matters to them.

Don't drop change announcements via email at 4.50 p.m. Friday - unless you're also announcing free puppies and cocktails. For clarity that would be two separate offers - I'm not suggesting the puppies would have cocktails. At any rate - pick your time for when your message will be heard, understood, engaged with and, ideally, positively received.

One-on-Ones that Actually Matter

Too many leaders treat 1:1s as optional - the first thing bumped for "urgent" tasks. That's like canceling dentist check-ups because you're too busy dealing with a toothache.

Tips for 1:1s:

- Show up on time - it signals respect.
- Ask more than you tell.

- Cover both the work and the human: "How's the project?" and "How are you holding up?"

- Close with clarity: "Here's what I'll do, here's what I need from you."

- Regular 1:1s shrink half the psychosocial hazards - low support, unclear expectations, and simmering conflict - before they flare up.

Critically though, follow through on any commitments you make so that the time is seen as valuable by both parties. The most common reason that we see for why 1:1's don't work is that people keep cancelling them. The second most common is that they are just a 'chat' and don't drive any action of behaviour. If you book the time, make sure it drives outcomes.

Meetings: Stop the Death by Powerpoint

To be fair I'm not aware of anyone actually dying from boring Powerpoint presentation, but I've seen some people get pretty close. If your meetings feel like death by Powerpoint (one person reading bullet-points out loud while everyone else scrolls their phone and tries not to absorb the boring), you don't have a meeting - you have a hostage situation.

- Send information ahead; use meeting time for decisions and discussion. If that doesn't happen it could have been an email.

- Keep them short, focused and, ideally, under the point where everyone's coffee wears off.

- End with: who's doing what by when - otherwise nothing just happened.

If you think you've communicated enough, say it three more times - then ask someone to repeat it back. Chances are they heard a slightly different story.

Mini Self-Scan

Score 1–5:

- I explain the why behind decisions before the rumour mill fills the gaps.
- I avoid jargon unless it actually saves time.
- My 1:1s happen consistently - not just when something's on fire.
- My meetings end with clear actions, not just calendar fatigue.
- I check for understanding instead of assuming my words were magic.

Communication is where most leaders accidentally lead like jerks - not because they mean to, but because silence, vagueness or jargon all feel like indifference on the receiving end.

Feedback Without the Flinch

Most leaders dread giving feedback almost as much as people dread receiving it. So they avoid it... until a small performance niggle grows teeth and needs an HR intervention.

Feedback is not a special occasion. It's leadership in its most basic form: "Here's what's working, here's what needs to change." It's also a two way street. Anyone who gives feedback must also be open to receiving it themself - without defensiveness, and ideally with a great deal of curiosity about how we can all be better. The more normal you make it, the less everyone flinches.

Why We Dodge It

Top four excuses we hear:

- "I don't want to hurt their feelings."
- "They already know they're struggling."
- "It'll be awkward."
- "They will weaponise it and use it against me."

Reality check: not giving feedback is the fastest way to hurt feelings, because you're silently letting someone fail. And yes, sometimes people do weaponise feedback. My view is that those people were likely looking for an in, and the more standardised and normalised feedback is in your organisation, the less legs those types of arguments have. Fear should not prevent us having honest discussions about performance, and how we can improve it as a team.

The 'No Surprises' Rule

No-one should ever walk into a formal performance review and discover something bad for the first time. That's not feedback - that's ambush. It's also entirely useless, as people are less likely to hear and accept it, and the time for effective intervention has probably passed.

Leaders who build a culture of no surprises:

- give bite-sized course-corrections in real time,
- balance positive with constructive so no one feels singled out,
- make praise specific: "Great job running that client call - you nailed the tough questions," not just "Good job."
- Scripts for the Tough Stuff

Here's a simple frame we teach in workshops - think of it as kind candour in four beats:

- Observation: "I noticed the report was two days late."
- Impact: "That pushed the whole team's schedule back."
- Expectation: "We need reports on time so we can hit client deadlines."
- Support / Next step: "What do you need to make that do-able next time?"

Short, specific, respectful - and not a lecture or moralising the issue. Just simply, that performance needs improvement because the organisation cannot function that way. What's in the way and what do we do in the future?

If you only give feedback once a year, don't be shocked when you get a year's worth of bad habits.

Feedback as a Trust-Builder

Done well, feedback is a sign of respect - it says, "I believe you can do better, and want to support you in doing that." Done badly, it's a scar. Leaders who offer clear, timely feedback reduce the psychosocial hazards of uncertainty and perceived unfairness, and they build trust instead of fear.

Mini Self-Scan

Score 1-5:

- I give positive feedback as specifically as I give corrective feedback.
- I address small performance dips early - before they become crises.
- My team knows what success looks like because I tell them.
- I ask what support they need rather than just pointing out what's wrong.
- My formal reviews contain no surprises.

Inclusion and Fairness in Daily Practice

You can't lead people well if only a few feel they belong and the rest feel like extras in someone else's movie.

Inclusion isn't just about diversity check-boxes; it's about how you run the day-to-day so everyone has a fair shot to do their best work.

Fair ≠ Identical

Leaders sometimes believe that treating everyone exactly the same is the fairest approach.

In reality, that often means treating everyone equally badly. Fairness means understanding that different people need different things to succeed:

- some thrive on public praise, others would rather walk across Lego than stand up in front of the team,
- some need a quiet space to think, others need to talk it out,
- some can stretch a deadline, others crumble if they don't know expectations up-front.

Your job isn't to create clones; it's to remove the friction that keeps people from performing. And including diverse viewpoints has been consistently shown to generate better quality ideas, more agile teams and more profitable organisations.

Spotting Everyday Bias Traps

Leaders often unintentionally reward:

- the loudest voice in meetings,
- the person who stays latest in the office,
- the one who talks a good game (even if delivery is patchy),
- the people who are most like themselves.

That sends an unspoken message to everyone else: "You don't count." A client once said to me, "The squeaky hinge gets the oil" - meaning that the people speaking up were the most valuable and should be given the most resources. I said to him - 'Or people can choose to use a different door.' We live in a society that values the extrovert, values visible busyness and values sameness. How these are not the things which make teams successful.

Left unchecked, it's a psychosocial hazard - perceived unfairness -

and it corrodes trust faster than a gossip-fuelled Slack thread.

Recognition Matters (More Than You Think)

Recognition isn't about handing out gold stars or pizza Fridays (although sometimes it is, but it doesn't have to be).

It's about noticing:

- the new analyst who quietly fixed a recurring system bug,
- the shift-lead who covered for someone's emergency without drama,
- the hybrid team member who dialled in at 6 a.m. from another time-zone because there was an urgent need

A simple, specific "I saw that - thank you" goes further than a gift card.

If your team only hears from you when something's wrong, you're not leading - you're lurking.

Fair Workload = Real Inclusion

Inclusion also means protecting people from chronic overload. If one person is the unofficial "go-to" for every urgent job because they always deliver, that's not a compliment - it's a slow-burn stress injury often referred to as a 'competency tax'.

Balanced work allocation, clear role boundaries, and predictable recognition aren't soft skills - they're core hazard controls.

Mini Self-Scan

Score 1-5:

- I notice and call out good work in real time, not just at review season.

- I spread opportunities fairly instead of defaulting to the same favourites.

- I ask quieter team members for input instead of letting louder voices dominate.

- I check workloads regularly to prevent chronic over-burdening.

- I challenge bias - including my own - when I spot it.

Leaders who practise daily fairness and inclusion see stronger trust, steadier engagement, and fewer grievances. It's not complicated - it's just often overlooked. Do this well and you remove one of the biggest psychosocial hazards hiding in plain sight.

Reflection Corner – Your People-Pillar Check-In

You've now read the good, the bad and the mildly ridiculous of leading humans. Before you charge into the next chapter, pause here and take stock. Leading people starts with noticing where you're already strong - and where you might be accidentally adding to the chaos.

Grab a pen, or the back of an old meeting agenda (no one ever looks at them again anyway), and score yourself.

Step 1 – Quick-Score on the People Basics

I = Needs work   3 = Passable   5 = Rock-solid

Leading Yourself

- I know my biggest stress-triggers and how they show up in my behaviour.
- I protect at least one non-negotiable daily boundary.
- My reactions stay consistent even under pressure - no "Monday me" vs "Thursday me."

Trust

- I do what I say I'll do - including the small promises.
- I explain the "why" behind decisions before the rumour mill fills the gaps.
- I'll apologise when I mess up, instead of quietly hoping no one noticed.

Communication

- My one-on-ones happen consistently, not just when something's on fire.
- My meetings end with clear actions and owners, not just calendar fatigue.
- I check that people actually understood the message - not just that I delivered it.

Feedback

- I give course-corrections early, in small doses, not as an annual ambush.

- I balance corrective feedback with specific positive recognition.
- My formal reviews contain no surprises.

Inclusion & Fairness

- I spread opportunities fairly instead of defaulting to the same favourites.
- I ask quieter voices for input instead of letting louder ones dominate.
- I notice and call out good work in real time.
- I monitor workload balance so no one silently burns out doing "just a bit more."

Step 2 – Find Your Lowest Pillar

Circle your lowest-scoring cluster.

That's probably where your jerk switch hides.

You don't have to fix everything overnight; start there.

Step 3 – One Small Move

Write down one small action you can take this week to strengthen that area.

(Example: schedule a skipped 1:1, clarify one role expectation, or simply thank someone for invisible work.)

You don't have to be everyone's favourite boss tomorrow. You just need to be a little less of a jerk today than you were yesterday.

Looking Ahead

You've just pressure-tested your People pillar. In the next chapter we'll tackle Proficiency - how to get the actual work done without chaos, drama or late-night emails labelled "quick favour."

Warm, trusting teams are great, however when missed deadlines and shifting priorities become the norm, all that effort to create that strong team is wasted in no time at all. Next we move to Proficiency: the habits and systems that keep the work flowing so your team's energy goes into progress, not just firefighting.

CHAPTER 4

GETTING STUFF DONE WITHOUT THE DRAMA

Thursday. 4:59 p.m.

Just as the team is closing laptops and someone is eyeing the pub across the road, an email pings:

Subject: URGENT - need numbers for the board pack tonight.

The sender? The same team leader who has had the report request in their inbox for a week. Cue the sound of collective groans and cancelled dinner plans.

By 5:15 the office looks like an episode of The Amazing Race:

- people frantically digging through spreadsheets,
- someone trying to remember what drove a half-finished pivot-table,

- two analysts arguing about whose version of the file is "the right one,"
- the team lead juggling Slack pings like a Vegas card-dealer.

This isn't a one-off emergency - it's every Thursday (and all the other days too if we're honest). Every week the team loses at least one evening to a last-minute "priority" that somehow no one planned for. And the drama of it is addictive.

The Cost of Chaos

The toll isn't just a few overtime pizzas:

- deadlines on the real work slip,
- quality tanks because everyone's rushing,
- resentment builds ("why bother planning if it's going to be blown up anyway"),
- people lose their ability to gauge how genuinely urgent a task is,
- good people quietly start looking for jobs with fewer "surprise" crises.

The business bleeds hours of productivity and goodwill. The humans burn out.

And it all comes from the same root cause: not lack of effort - lack of Proficiency.

Drama like this isn't a personality trait of the team; it's usually a systems failure:

- priorities unclear,
- decision rights fuzzy,
- processes either absent or ignored.

If the People pillar is about how we treat each other, Proficiency is about how we organise the work.

Get it wrong and you don't just create inefficiency - you create psychosocial hazards: constant high demand, role conflict, the stress of living on red alert. This is completely unsustainable for any of us. And the performance erosion compounds over time - so when left unchecked you can find yourself with a pretty steep incline back to productivity.

This chapter is about taming that chaos so your team can get stuff done - without the late-night pizza and the slow leak of goodwill.

Why Proficiency Matters

Most teams don't fail because the humans suddenly forgot how to work. They fail because the work isn't organised in a way that lets them succeed. We like to think drama comes from "difficult personalities."

More often, it comes from:

- priorities that change every week (or every hour),
- decisions stuck in inbox limbo,
- processes that exist only on slide 47 of a forgotten presentation,
- leaders assuming "people will just figure it out."

That's not a people problem. That's a Proficiency problem - the missing piece between good strategy and good execution.

The DLPA Lens

People is about how we treat the humans. Profit is about the results we're here to deliver.

Proficiency is how we turn good intentions into finished work - without the drama.

It's the habits, systems and clarity that stop your team's energy leaking into re-work, waiting, firefighting and stress.

The Human Cost of Low Proficiency

Poor Proficiency isn't just inefficient - it's hazardous. We see the same psychosocial hazards flare up again and again:

- High job demand - constant urgent work and no breathing space.
- Role conflict - two people doing the same task, or worse, no one doing it at all.
- Low control - decisions sit with the wrong level or never get made.
- Unpredictability - last-minute changes undo a week of careful planning.

These don't just tank productivity; they fry people's nervous systems. Chronic confusion is as stressful as chronic overwork, if not more so.

The Business Cost of Chaos

Organisations with low Proficiency pay what we call the Chaos Tax:

- projects drag or stall,
- customer deadlines get missed,
- overtime balloons while output stays flat,
- change fatigue sets in,
- turnover climbs because the best people don't stick around for the circus.

That's money, morale and reputation leaking out of the business - quietly, every day.

Proficiency isn't bureaucracy. It's the difference between a Formula 1 pit stop and a clown car with a flat tyre.

In the next section we'll name the five most common Drama Traps that destroy Proficiency - so you can spot them in your own world before they cost you the weekend.

Diagnosing the Drama Traps

If Proficiency is about how we organise the work, then drama is what fills the vacuum when that structure is missing. Below are the five traps we see most often when teams struggle to get stuff done.

1. Priority Confetti

Symptom:

Everything is a top priority - until tomorrow, when there's a new top priority.

Example:

A marketing team we worked with had 19 "mission-critical" projects. By the end of Q2, only three were finished - without any KPI's actually being met. The rest limped along half-done because nobody knew which to sacrifice, or which to focus on.

Human Cost:

People stop trying to prioritise, morale dives, and resentment builds ("Why bother planning when it all changes next week?"). When everything is urgent, nothing really gets done. People lose their ability to even engage in any form of triaging, and tasks all meld into each other. Value is a foreign concept and everything is about effort.

Proficiency Fix:

Pick a maximum of three genuine priorities at a time and park the rest. Yes, only three. A clear "not now" list is as important as the to-do list. You can of course maintain the chute and have a pipeline of needs coming, but urgent priorities can only ever be three.

2. Decision Bottlenecks

Symptom:

Every sign-off gets stuck with the same over-busy executive or committee. Decisions when or if they come are no longer relevant.

Example:

We saw a construction project where tile samples sat in a GM's office for three weeks waiting for approval. The project was delayed

- not by weather or ground conditions, but by one person's decision stagnation. In this example it wasn't that the GM was deliberately procrastinating or delaying the decision. He felt so paralysed by the sheer volume of decisions he was having to make, without any real structure on how, that he found himself oscillating and never reaching the point of decisiveness.

Human Cost:

Teams stall, deadlines slip, blame games start, and staff feel powerless. Rogue players start making decisions - often poor quality ones - just to keep the ball rolling. Any semblance of governance or process falls and predictability in the environment plummets.

Proficiency Fix:

Push decisions down to the lowest sensible level and make roles and decision rights explicit. Give people a framework to make good quality decisions quickly, within their scope and delegation. Equip your team to be able to recognise competitive advantage and how to compound it with their decisions, and give them the structure to move with agility.

"A decision stuck in email limbo is like wet cement - the longer it sits, the harder it is to move.

3. Zombie Projects

Symptom:

Projects that nobody remembers why they started, but nobody wants to kill. There's no end date, no real point, but everyone just keeps plugging away.

Example:

In a financial-services client, a "customer-journey dashboard" soaked up six figures of budget for 18 months - and was never actually launched. No one could explain the original business case, and people had forgotten what actions the 'insights' were going to drive. The project seems pretty removed from the customers.

Human Cost:

Zombie work sucks time, focus and goodwill from everything that still matters. They aren't energising, and the longer we keep giving them oxygen the more distant we are from the real strategy. Once we disconnect from the strategy whether or not we add value with our actions is pure chance.

Proficiency Fix:

Do quarterly project amnesties: kill or close anything that no longer serves a clear business or customer need. Map the timeline to deliverables, connected to strategic outcomes. Celebrate the wins as you go to keep people engaged with the project. And if needs change, never be afraid to say 'this doesn't serve us anymore'. The small caveat here is to ensure that you always honor the work that has gone before. People can be very demoralised if their projects are killed and they have spent a lot of energy and emotional investment on them. Keeping people connected to the strategic relevance is the key.

Zombie projects don't just eat brains - they eat budgets.

4. Process by PowerPoint

Symptom:

Processes exist in slides, manuals or SharePoint folders - but not in daily practice. Processes are something you show the auditor, not new hires. Processes describe an aspirational ideal world which is completely different from the organisation.

Example:

A hybrid tech team had a gorgeous 30-page "agile ways-of-working" deck. It looked stunning, had interactive elements, multiple models and clean process maps showing everyone's swim lanes and how they interrelated. Turns out only two people had ever opened it, zero had fully read it and none of the rituals were happening.

Human Cost:

Teams waste time reinventing the wheel and blaming each other for missed steps. There is mass confusion about who is supposed to be doing what. There is a culture of trying to hide a 'secret' at audit time and pretend the procedures are real - which is exhausting. People make up their own procedures and silos flourish.

Proficiency Fix:

Keep processes visible, real and simple. Embed them in the workflow, not in the archive.

Train new starters on the real process, not the slide. Let feedback flow back through so that processes evolve with your company and become tools of agility, not barriers to productivity.

5. Fire-Drill Culture

Symptom:

Constant reactive scramble; yesterday's emergencies hijack today's plans.

Example:

An operations team we worked with proudly called themselves "ninja firefighters." They were busy, heroic - and exhausted. They were really proud of their ability to react quickly to crises and deal with the unexpected. However, customer complaints were creeping up because the core work kept getting bumped for the latest drama. What's more, they couldn't see how their addiction to firefighting meant that they were unable to properly engage with business as usual. They were so reactive they had no skill or awareness of pro-active action. They were so busy looking for the next fire, they completely missed the present opportunities.

Human Cost:

Burnout, errors, endless overtime, rising turnover. These high stress environments actually reduce possible cognitive load over time - meaning that the longer this goes on the less ability workers have to actually process or even recognise new information (yet alone form new ideas). This leads to dangerous assumption creep, constant panic and confusion, and eventually disengagement.

Proficiency Fix:

Separate real emergencies from poor planning. Block "quiet hours" for focus work, and build a weekly prioritisation cadence that everyone trusts. If required, bring in a short term contingent workforce with a tight remit to get things back on track. Actively build the team's skillset in scanning for opportunities, focusing on strategic work, and identifying the early signs that a crisis may be coming.

Being great at firefighting isn't a strategy, it's just proof you live in a tinderbox.

Each of these traps is a signal that Proficiency is missing in action. Fix the underlying system - clarity, priorities, decision paths, simple processes - and the drama dies down.

Next, we'll look at the Building Blocks of Proficiency: practical habits that keep work flowing smoothly so you don't spend Fridays putting out fires you accidentally lit on Monday.

Building Blocks of Proficiency

Proficiency isn't red tape. It's the scaffolding that lets good people do good work without tripping over each other or themselves. Below are the core habits that separate a busy team from a productive one.

1. Clarity First: Define Success Up-Front

Vague goals breed vague effort. If you want work delivered on time, you have to tell people:

- What's expected: plain-language outcome, not just a slogan.
- By when: not "ASAP", rather an actual date.

- How we'll measure success: so there's no "surely this is good enough."

FYI: 'ASAP' is not a deadline; it's a mood.

2. Decision Rights: Who Decides What

Teams stall when everyone thinks someone else is deciding. Write it down: who approves budgets, who green-lights changes, who kills a zombie project.

A simple RACI (Responsible, Accountable, Consulted, Informed) chart on one page beats a 20-page governance manual that nobody reads. A team without clear decision rights is just a group of people huddled together hoping for the best. To thrive, teams must know who can decide what, and within what framework.

3. Simple Systems: Make the Right Way the Easy Way

Most people don't hate process; they hate pointless, clunky process that makes their job harder.

Good systems:

- are as short as they possibly can be whilst still being clear,
- live where the work happens (e.g. in the workflow tool, not in an old PDF or actual dusty folder),
- save time rather than add it.

Example: A three-question quality checklist can prevent five emails and a re-work loop later.

4. Close the Loop: Track, Review, Adjust

Leaders often launch an initiative then move on, assuming it'll run itself. It rarely does. Weekly 10-minute check-ins on progress, obstacles and next steps keep things from drifting into zombie-land. Close the loop in meetings, too: finish every discussion with "who's doing what by when" so no one leaves guessing.

Then, make sure you review. Hold people accountable to what they said they would do. Don't tolerate constant deadline slippage. Review the outputs, hold people accountable, take the feedback and adjust and refine as you go.

5. Meetings That Move Work Forward

We covered People-pillar basics for 1:1s; now for delivery meetings:

- Send information before the meeting - don't read slides at people. Give them time to prepare, and expect them to turn up prepared.
- Keep them short and focused: decisions and blockers, not status theatre or show and tell.
- Use a visible action list: no action = no meeting. And visibly check in on progress too.

Golden rule: If it could have been an email, it should have been an email.

6. Change Without Chaos

Change is inevitable; chaos is optional. When you roll out a new tool, process or structure:

- Explain the why first, in plain language and linked to people's day-to-day.
- Test it small, pilot with one team, learn, then scale.
- Train & support, don't assume a single email will do it or that people will accept it straight away.
- De-commission the old way, or people will keep doing both.

A thoughtful change plan reduces the psychosocial hazards of uncertainty, overload and this-too-shall-pass cynicism.

7. Make Progress Visible

People stay motivated when they can see progress. A simple shared dashboard or kanban board helps everyone know what's done, what's stuck, and what's next. This means fewer "just-checking-in" emails, more autonomy. Whilst some of the visualisation tools have been overdone, that is only because the base idea is so effective. When people can see the progress of a project, and the different sections moving forward they understand resource allocation better, are able to prioritise better and momentum builds. A very simple display can be a fundamental cultural shift.

Proficiency isn't about more paperwork; it's about removing friction so the work flows:

- clear priorities,
- clear decision-paths,
- simple systems,
- tight feedback loops.

Done well, it keeps your team out of the five Drama Traps, and keeps you out of the Friday night fire-drill.

Next up: we'll look at "Change-Management Without the Eye-Roll" and how to introduce new ways of working so people don't dig in their heels or quietly wait for it to blow over.

Change-Management Without the Eye-Roll

The words "We're rolling out a change..." are enough to make half a workforce reach for their stress-ball or fidget spinner. Not because people hate progress - though, let's be honest, some do - but because they've lived through too many half-baked roll-outs that created more pain than progress, only to fizzle out and have delivery teams desperately try to erase that the project ever existed.

Change itself isn't the hazard. Poorly handled change is.

Why Change Hurts

Most change trips three predictable psychosocial hazards:

- Uncertainty: "Will this make my job harder or obsolete?"
- Loss of control: decisions are made somewhere far away and dropped on people like a memo from the clouds.
- Workload spike: leaders forget that learning new systems or processes is extra work on top of the day-job, and often reduces cognitive load overall.

Add patchy communication and you have the perfect recipe for rumour-mill panic, burnout and disengagement.

The DLPA Way: Treat Change as a People Project

At DLPA we tell clients:

"Every operational change is also a people-project - ignore that and you'll buy yourself a resistance movement, and guarantee yourself a failed project."

Our golden rule: context before content.

Explain why the change matters to the organisation and to each person's day-to-day reality before you unleash the slide deck. Not high level, pie in the sky ideas. What is the change and why should they care?

Four Habits of Change that Actually Sticks

Start with the Why-For-Them

Not a lofty vision statement. Spell out how it makes their work easier, safer, better, more enriching or more valuable to customers.

Shrink the Unknowns

Outline what's staying the same as clearly as what's changing - predictability calms the lizard brain. Reassure that you have thought through the impact and know how to protect what's valuable.

Stage, Don't Dump

A construction firm wanted to modernise their project management. They bought a brilliant digital platform - scheduling, procurement, on-site updates, client dashboards - the works. Then someone decided to "de-risk" the rollout by launching only the scheduling module first. Except scheduling fed procurement which fed inventory which fed the on-site updates. By launching half, they snapped the plumbing.

Within two weeks the site teams were running dual systems: the new schedule for show, the old spreadsheet for sanity. Procurement requests went missing because they weren't triggered by the right status code. Supervisors were yelled at for not updating "the system" that didn't actually talk to the other system. A project engineer said, "It's like we replaced the engine and left the car on bricks."

Morale dipped. People quietly invented workarounds. The platform vendor got blamed (unfairly). The project was on the brink of becoming another cautionary slide titled "Why Tech Fails Here."

We paused the rollout and did something radical: treated it as a people-project. First, we mapped the end-to-end workflow on a literal wall. Where does information start? Who touches it? When does a step become a dependency? That map made one truth obvious: launching one module in isolation broke the chain of custody. Second, we ran a two-week pilot on two sites with the full stack. Small scope, high support, instant feedback loops. Third, we trained supervisors on the "why-for-them": fewer double-entries, faster approvals, less midnight Excel archaeology.

Guess what happened? The system didn't become perfect - the work did become doable. People stopped inventing shadow processes. "Change fatigue" melted when the change saved time. And because we killed the halfway house, there was no more political cover to blame the software for design errors.

Here's the Proficiency pillar in one sentence: design the work so the right way is the easy way. If your "staged rollout" makes the right way impossible, it isn't a stage, it's a stall. And stalls breed cynicism.

Pilot where you can. Introduce one behaviour at a time. Nothing says "we don't get it" like twelve new log-ins launched on the same Monday. And one change gone wrong is much easier to roll back than twelve.

Keep Feedback Loops Alive

Give people a way to flag issues early (and actually respond to them). A ten-minute stand-up to ask "what's clunky?" can save weeks of silent sabotage. Let people tell you how they are experiencing a change so that you can either refine it, adjust the course or explain why things are the way they are.

A Quick Story: The Policy That Went Poof

A client once issued a brand-new hybrid-work policy by email late on a Friday (you already know this is going badly). To be fair it was in the heart of COVID-19 times and we were all making a series of really bad decisions. At any rate, by Monday there were three versions floating around Slack, none of them the real one. The first staff Q&A turned into a therapy session filled with hysteria. The policy was pulled and we started working a Take Two.

When we re-launched:

- the leader opened with why the change mattered to staff as well as the business,

- managers were briefed first so they could field questions and could explain the policy more fully before the gossip started up,
- we ditched jargon and answered the "what stays the same" question up-front,
- and we hosted informal huddles to iron out kinks in the first month.

Resistance dropped to almost nothing - because we treated it like a people-project, not an all-staff email or policy rollout.

Most people don't resist change - they resist being surprised and confused by change.

Handled well, change doesn't have to spike stress or productivity dips. Handled badly, it fuels the drama traps of priority-confetti, fire-drills and morale crashes.

Proficiency-minded leaders remember that processes don't adopt themselves - people do. And a process is only ever as valuable as the actions of the people following it. Your job is to make that adoption as painless, predictable and purposeful as possible.

Metrics That Matter

Leaders love numbers. Unfortunately, they often fall in love with the wrong ones - the shiny dashboard dials that look important in a board pack but tell you nothing about whether work is actually getting done. To be honest, sometimes even better if they don't. Those more insightful numbers can lead to awkward conversations.

Some leaders will stare at charts the way teenagers stare at TikTok: hypnotised, mildly entertained... and no wiser than before and maybe just a little dumber.

Vanity Metrics vs. Useful Metrics

Vanity metrics are like empty calories: they look good, feel satisfying, but do nothing to keep the business alive.

Think:

- number of meetings or briefings (spoiler: more meetings rarely equals more progress),
- number of slides produced,
- how many "hearts" or "stars" a new initiative announcement got on the intranet.

Useful metrics answer three boring but crucial questions:

1. Are we getting the right things done?
2. Are we doing them well and on time?
3. Can we keep it up without breaking the humans or the business?

Three Buckets That Actually Matter

Flow Metrics – Is the work moving or stuck in limbo?

Lead-time, cycle-time, on-time delivery, how fast blockers get cleared, how quickly do we respond to customers, where is there drag.

Quality Metrics – Is it any good or will we redo it next week?

Error rates, re-work volume, first-time-right %, customer complaints, warranty claims, nonconformances.

Capacity & Health Metrics – Can the humans keep this up?

Overtime hours, unplanned absenteeism, staff turnover, survey items about workload and clarity, engagement with EAPs and wellness programs.

If you don't measure the strain on the humans, you're just counting widgets until the widgets quit.

The Psychosocial Safety Link

Teams notice what you measure. If all you track is speed and volume, don't be shocked when quality dips and people quietly burn out. Balancing output with re-work and capacity metrics says: "We care about results and keeping you in one piece."

A Quick Story: The Busy-But-Broken Team

One client's operations team proudly hit 95 % "billable utilisation" every month. On paper they looked like rockstars; in reality they were exhausted... and the margins were going south.

Why?

They were re-doing the same jobs twice. Fire-drills kept pushing other deadlines late. Two top performers were working heroic unpaid overtime - right up until they handed in their resignations.

We swapped out their vanity KPI for ones that included re-work rate, cycle-time, and planned-vs-unplanned overtime. Two quarters later, profits rose and the Sunday-night email panic halved.

If you only measure how fast the hamster wheel spins, don't be surprised when the hamster keels over.

The right metrics don't just decorate a dashboard; they change behaviour. A Proficiency-minded leader tracks how the work flows, whether it lands the first time, and whether the people doing it can still walk upright at the end of the week. Everything else is corporate glitter.

Reflection Corner – Your Proficiency Pulse Check

You've survived the drama traps and the hamster-wheel talk. Now it's time to see where your own systems are helping...or secretly sabotaging you.

Grab whatever's handy - a notebook, a napkin, the back of last week's meeting agenda (the one nobody read) - and do a quick pulse-check.

Step 1 – Quick-Score on the Proficiency Basics

1 = Needs work   3 = Passable   5 = Rock-solid

Priorities

- We keep no more than three clear priorities at a time - everyone can name them without checking a deck.
- We have a visible "not-now" list so we're not juggling 15 shiny objects at once.

Decision-Making

- People know who decides what - no mysteries, no email limbo.

- Routine decisions get made at the lowest sensible level, not always by the busiest executive.

Systems & Processes

- The "real" process lives where the work happens, not just in a dusty PDF.

- Hand-overs are smooth - no recurring "I thought you were doing that" moments.

- Projects either move or get killed; we don't feed zombie work.

Meetings & Follow-Through

- Most meetings end with "who's doing what by when" instead of calendar fatigue.

- We send info before meetings so we don't waste time reading slides at each other.

- We close the loop on initiatives - we don't launch and walk away.

Change & Capacity

- We roll out change with context first so people understand the why-for-them.

- We stage and pilot major changes instead of dumping twelve new log-ins on Monday morning.

- We track workload health (overtime, re-work, churn) as well as delivery stats.

Step 2 – Spot Your Drama Trap

Look for your lowest-scoring cluster. That's usually where the chaos is sneaking in: maybe decision bottlenecks, maybe priority confetti, maybe meetings that should've been emails.

Step 3 – Pick One Fix-It Move

Write down one small change you can try this week:

- Kill or park one zombie project.
- Post a "not-now" list.
- Add a 10-minute Friday check-in to clear blockers.
- Or simply start finishing every meeting with "who's doing what by when."

You don't have to rebuild your whole operating system overnight - just patch the bug that keeps crashing your week.

Looking Ahead

You've now pressure-tested your Proficiency pillar - the engine-room of getting stuff done.

Next, we'll climb the last pillar of the DLPA model: Profit - how to align all that effort with the business results that keep the lights on (and maybe even pay for better coffee).

CHAPTER 5

PROFIT: MAKING THE WORK ACTUALLY PAY OFF

The Perfect Project that Changed Nothing

Six months. Three cross-functional workshops. A war-room plastered in sticky-notes, colour-coded timelines, two separate steering committees and (at one point) a celebratory cake that said "Phase One Complete!"

The project was delivered on time, on budget, with flawless reports. Everyone got shiny slide decks for the board pack, the executive sponsor got a LinkedIn brag post, and the project manager went on holiday convinced they'd just saved the company. High fives all round.

Only one small hitch: it didn't change a single business outcome. Revenue didn't budge. Customer complaints didn't drop. Staff were still drowning in the same clunky system they'd been promised would be "streamlined."

What looked like success on the Gantt chart turned out to be just a very expensive team-building exercise with worse catering.

Why This Happens

We see versions of this story in nearly every organisation:

- Brilliant delivery on things that don't move the scoreboard.

- Teams exhausting themselves chasing KPIs that look good on a slidedeck but don't pay the bills.

- Leaders proudly saying, "We hit every milestone!" while Finance quietly points at a flat line on the P&L.

It's not that people are lazy or clueless - they're often excellent at their craft. What's missing is the Profit pillar of leadership: knowing how the business actually wins and making sure the team's effort lines up with that.

If your big win doesn't change a line on the P&L or make a customer happier, it's not a transformation - it's an expensive hobby.

This chapter is about that third DLPA pillar: Profit.

Not spreadsheets-for-spreadsheets'-sake, but understanding the commercial levers that keep the lights on, the coffee machine running, and the wages paid. For NFP's and Government we sometimes get a bit of resistance to this pillar. A client said it best, "Whilst we are not for profit, we equally aren't for loss." Profit does not need to mean huge corporate conglomerates eating baby seals off ivory tables. Profit, in this context, means the fundamental organisational levers which mean your balance sheet balances. Whether you choose to use that benefit to increase your impact, or buy another super yacht, is a matter for your organisation.

And remember, no matter how healthy your People pillar or how slick your Proficiency pillar, if the work doesn't connect to the organisation's real value drivers, you're just running a very enthusiastic hamster wheel with nowhere to go.

Profit-blind leaders often become accidental jerks

Not because they're mean-spirited, but because when the money doesn't line up with the mission, they start making panicked, short-sighted calls: cancelling projects overnight, freezing budgets mid-stream, blaming Finance for bad news. Nothing frays trust or morale faster than a leader who feels out of their depth with the numbers and over-corrects by becoming reactive or controlling.

If you want to avoid that jerk spiral, you have to know enough about the commercial levers to stay calm, explain the trade-offs, and keep your team focused on what actually pays the bills.

What 'Profit' Really Means

A surprising number of leaders treat Profit as if it's something that lives exclusively in Finance - like it's locked away in a spreadsheet vault guarded by accountants with green visors. That's a problem, because every decision in every department either feeds profit or leaks it.

Profit in the DLPA model isn't about stock-price hype or corporate swagger. It's about the commercial levers that keep the organisation alive:

- the income that funds the mission,
- the margins that pay for staff, tools and coffee,
- the efficiency that lets you reinvest or serve more people next year than you did last year.

Not Just for the Private Sector

A surprising number of leaders still think "Profit" is Finance's private business - something that lives in mysterious spreadsheets behind a locked office door. But every leader, in every department, affects the money.

In the DLPA model, Profit simply means financial sustainability: the money that keeps the lights on, the coffee machine stocked, the wages paid, and the mission funded.

You don't have to become an accountant, but you do have to understand which levers drive your part of the business: revenue, cost, efficiency, risk and customer value. Ignore those, and even the best People and Proficiency work will be like pouring water into a bucket with a hole in the bottom.

Profit-savvy leaders don't see budgets as red tape; they see them as guardrails. They use them to make smarter trade-offs, explain the 'why' behind decisions to their teams, and spot the slow leaks that sink strategy long before Finance sends the dreaded email.

The Leadership Gap

Many technical leaders rise through the ranks brilliant at their craft but with little exposure to the commercial side.

That often leads to:

- well-intended projects that don't move the organisational scoreboard,
- gold-plated solutions for problems customers didn't want solved,
- heroic efforts that win awards but not repeat business.

That's not incompetence; it's context blindness. You can't steer the ship if you don't know where the harbour is.

Why It Matters

Understanding Profit gives leaders:

- the ability to prioritise the work that actually funds the mission,
- the language to advocate for resources credibly,
- the context to explain the 'why' behind tough trade-offs to their teams,
- and the radar to spot waste and hidden cost-leaks before Finance sends the dreaded spreadsheet.

Profit-savvy leaders make better day-to-day calls - which protects the People and Proficiency pillars from chronic "do-more-with-less" stress.

The Cost of Leading Blind

It turns out blowing the budget takes no special qualification - just enthusiasm and a lack of visibility.

The pattern is painfully familiar:

- A well-intentioned leader launches a "must-have" initiative with no idea how it'll be funded, or how it will pay that funding back.

- A team keeps hiring "just one more" contractor because the backlog feels urgent.

- A manager approves every training request because it feels mean to say no.

- Or the reverse: they slash spending on something invisible (like preventative maintenance) and then act surprised when the roof literally caves in.

None of these leaders set out to sabotage the business. They just weren't taught to read the financial weather.

When you don't know the commercial levers:

- You chase shiny things that don't move the dial.
- You pinch pennies that cost dollars later.
- You over-service clients who aren't actually profitable (the "favourite child" account that secretly drains margin).
- You under-invest in the quiet work that protects the balance sheet - risk controls, maintenance, skills development.

The damage doesn't always show up straight away; it sneaks in as slow leaks: margin erosion, ballooning overtime, rising churn, balloon-and-burst budgets.

I once worked with a division head who proudly declared, "We smashed our revenue target this quarter!"

True - but she'd also doubled the discount rate to win sales. The top line looked fantastic; the bottom line looked like a horror film. And worse - now the market was being educated that this company would discount. This small action taken to 'smash' revenue targets, did huge damage to the business for a very long time.

Profit blindness isn't just a Finance headache - it's a leadership hazard. Leaders who don't understand the money often end up leading like jerks: promising what they can't fund, yanking resources at the last minute, or blaming the team for gaps they never saw coming. It drives short-term heroics at the expense of long-term health, feeds constant "cost-cutting surprises," and demoralises teams who never understand why yesterday's 'urgent priority' is today's cancelled project.

Lesson:

If you don't understand how your team's work hits the P&L, you're steering with the headlights off. You might still make progress... until you find the cliff.

Levers Every Leader Should Know

You don't need to memorise the entire P&L to lead for Profit - you just need to know which handful of levers your decisions actually pull. Think of them as the four gears every leader can reach without calling Finance.

1. Revenue: Where the Money Comes From

Not just "sales." Revenue is influenced by every department that touches the customer experience:

- Service teams who keep clients renewing.
- Project leads who stop scope-creep from turning a fixed-price job into a charity project.
- Front-line staff who upsell or cross-sell because they understand what the customer really needs.

Leader's role: know your main revenue streams and what behaviours in your team grow or shrink them. If you don't know what makes money, you can't prioritise the work that protects it.

2. Cost & Waste: Where the Money Leaks

Costs aren't just in the procurement system. Leaders leak money every day by tolerating re-work, endless approval loops, idle downtime, and over-servicing "favourite" clients.

Leader's role: hunt the slow leaks - not just the big capital spend but the thousand tiny drips that flatten margins. A culture that celebrates firefighting over planning is usually hiding a cost leak somewhere.

3. Risk: The Quiet Profit Eater

Most leaders only think of risk when something's already gone wrong and someone's yelling about compliance. But unmanaged risk - safety, psychosocial, legal, brand - is just deferred cost.

Leader's role: spot the hazards early. Build in small controls (boundaries, clear roles, solid processes) before they turn into a media headline or a lawsuit. Risk-savvy leaders protect both people and profit.

4. Customer Value: The Profit Multiplier

Not all customers are created equal. Some pay on time, stay loyal, and grow with you.

Others keep you busy for free. Quite good of them really.

Leader's role: know which customers or services add value, which don't, and steer your team's effort accordingly. Over-servicing the wrong customer is one of the fastest ways to look busy and go broke.

The Point:

You don't have to run the spreadsheets - but if you don't understand these levers, you'll make decisions that accidentally choke revenue, inflate costs, or load up risk.

Profit-minded leaders keep these four gears in view so they can align their team's effort with the organisation's real value drivers.

Drama-Free Budget Conversations

For many leaders, talking about money with their teams feels like discussing politics at Christmas lunch: awkward, full of landmines, and guaranteed to raise someone's blood pressure.

But dodging the topic only makes it worse. When leaders clam up about money, the rumour mill fills the void - and that's when the 'jerk boss' stories start.:

"Management's cutting costs again because they're greedy" or

"Profits must be huge, so why can't we get more staff?"

A few principles make budget talk less terrifying - and more useful.

1. Speak Human, Not Spreadsheet

Nothing kills attention faster than opening with EBITDA margins or CapEx ratios.

Translate the numbers into what matters for their world:

- "Every late job costs us $1,200 in overtime."
- "Every extra day on that project means we pay for another crane."
- "This client's discount means we're basically delivering the last week for free."

If the team can't see the link between their daily decisions and the dollars, the message won't stick.

2. Explain the Trade-Offs

Budgets aren't just about saying no; they're about choosing what matters most.

Frame it as priorities:

"We can fund the extra training OR the new equipment this quarter

- which one helps us hit the target fastest?"

Inviting the team into the trade-offs not only surfaces better ideas, it builds trust that the process isn't just bean-counting. In order to effectively engage with the concept of profit, teams must understand that it is finite, and that there is a constant balance about how to get the most out of the budget you have.

3. Kill the Mystery Budget Line

Every workplace has that one cost nobody understands - "Overheads," "On Costs", "Shared Services," or my personal favourite, "Miscellaneous" (sometimes also called "Prelims").

Clarify where the money goes. Transparency defuses a lot of the 'us vs. them' resentment. It is a very rare thing for departments to be actively ripping each other off. Have a consistent narrative across the company for where the money goes, and what the organisation needs in return for the spend. No black holes!

4. Make Wins Visible

Celebrate when smart decisions save costs or grow margin. A quiet email from Finance saying "well done" isn't enough - share the story so the team sees that their choices really do move the dial, and in what way. This also helps develop the playbook for how the organisation can routinely exceed targets and can constantly find better ways of doing things.

5. Stay Calm When the Math Hurts

Budget shortfalls can trigger defensiveness or finger-pointing. Model the tone you want: factual, not fearful; solutions, not scapegoats. A leader who panics about the budget teaches everyone else to panic, too. There is no emotion in a budget, so when it goes wrong if you keep the focus on problem-solving and learning, the team will learn to interact this way too.

Bottom line:

Money conversations don't have to be grim lectures in spreadsheet hieroglyphics. Done well, they're just part of explaining the 'why' behind decisions - the same skill you use to lead People and Proficiency. The goal isn't to turn your team into accountants; it's to help them understand how their daily decisions feed (or drain) the bigger picture.

Common Profit Myths That Sink Teams

Leaders rarely set out to be careless with money. But they often run on half-baked assumptions that quietly wreck both morale and margin. Here are the greatest hits we see on repeat:

1. "Revenue Fixes Everything"

More sales are great - unless they're unprofitable. Unprofitable sales mean you are literally paying someone to do work for them. Other than if you are engaged in an aggressive market share grab (I'll save my personal views of that tactic for a quiet chat with a nice wine), this cannot possibly make sense for an organisation. Surely you would rather sit on a beach for free and not worry about the stress of it? We've seen teams celebrate record-breaking sales months while quietly losing money on every deal because of discounts (often unsolicited discounts), re-work and free extras.

Reality check: Revenue is just the front door; profit leaks out the back if you don't watch costs, scope and delivery quality.

2. *"Cutting Costs = Cutting Corners"*

Some leaders think every cost cut is an act of cruelty - others think every cut is a hero move.

Both are wrong. Killing waste (duplicate systems, zombie projects, endless firefighting) is smart.

Killing investments that protect people, quality or competitive advantage is a false economy that usually costs more later. It also endangers the organisation's future. Rather than 'cutting costs' we encourage organisations to think in terms of 'getting more bang for buck'. Not how can I spend less, but rather how can I get more from what I spend.

3. *"Budget = Finance's Problem"*

The number of leaders who shrug and say "Finance handles that" is alarming. If your decisions spend or save money (spoiler: almost all do) it's your problem, too. Delegating budget thinking to Finance is like delegating your driving to the GPS: you'll still hit the tree if you don't steer. Finance usually knows where you are trying to go, but only you can take the actions to get there.

4. *"If It's Not in the KPI, It Doesn't Matter"*

Metrics are essential - but they're not and should not be scripture. Leaders who chase the KPI at the expense of common sense (like over-servicing a client to hit a volume target) often hit the number while missing the point (and the profit). Well crafted KPI's provide the framework and signposts. They shouldn't be viewed as an exhaustive list of tasks or points of focus.

5. "Good Service Always Pays for Itself"

Great service is worth it - but only if it's priced or resourced to match. If your strategy is competing on price, service ultimately just needs to be good enough. Over-delivering for free may win hearts, but it drains the budget and burns out staff. A leader's job is to make sure generosity has a sustainable business case.

The Fix:

Profit-minded leaders challenge these myths in themselves and in their teams.

They ask: "Does this choice actually add value - or just make us feel busy or virtuous?"

Knowing the difference is what keeps the lights on and the team engaged.

Profit Signals Every Leader Should Watch

You don't need a degree in corporate finance or a 50-slide dashboard. You just need to keep an eye on a few signals that tell you whether the business is healthy or springing leaks.

Think of these as the lights on your car's dashboard: if you ignore them, don't act surprised when smoke pours out of the bonnet halfway down the highway.

We ran a DLPA intensive for a large government agency - fifty leaders, decent-ish coffee, and the usual pre-workshop murmurs about "why Finance makes everything so confusing." On day two, during a break, a senior executive lingered as the room emptied. He'd been in the public service for over twenty years, held a sprawling portfolio, and had that calm, seen-it-all presence. He said, barely above a whisper, "I don't actually know how to read the budget properly."

He didn't mean he couldn't skim the headlines. He meant he didn't really understand the mechanics - margin erosion, accrual timing, what a variance should trigger in day-to-day decisions. For years he'd surfed the summaries, smiled through Finance updates, and relied on a very patient director to translate. He'd never asked for help because he thought the laughter would echo forever down the corridors.

So we pulled up a chair. Ten minutes on revenue vs. cost-to-serve, why cash timing and accruals are different cousins, the simplest way to spot a leak (re-work, overtime, discounts, scope creep). Another ten on reading a P&L line-by-line like a story instead of a riddle: "What changed? Is it a one-off or a pattern? Whose behaviour touches this number?" We sketched a tiny 'cheat grid': margin per service line, re-work cost, overtime trend, top five late payers. No acronyms Olympics, no judgement.

He came back after lunch to a different man. Not because he'd become Warren Buffett - because shame had been replaced by curiosity. Within a week he'd started a 20-minute "money huddle" with his directors. Each month they'd look at five signals and pick one to fix. First month: re-work on a particular program had crept up. Turned out the team was copying old templates that no longer matched policy. One updated checklist later, re-work halved. Second month: overtime was disguising a vacancy no one had the energy to recruit for. They hired. Overtime fell. People slept. The budget breathed.

The revelation for him wasn't the math. It was the permission. He didn't need to be a finance savant - he needed enough literacy to ask the right questions and the psychological safety to admit he didn't know. That's the Profit pillar at work: not spreadsheets-for-spreadsheets'-sake, but clarity that helps leaders steer.

1. Margin per Project / Product

Top-line revenue is the party selfie; margin is the morning-after bank balance. If the margin on what you sell keeps shrinking, you're working harder for less return. Leaders should know at least roughly: "For every dollar we bring in here, how much do we keep?" If there is a loss-leading style strategy (again, not endorsed but they certainly do exist), you still need to understand what that loss is and should be, so you can balance if that 'investment' is worth it.

2. Cost-to-Serve

Some customers or products are secretly loss-leaders because of hidden extras: extra meetings, rush jobs, hand-holding or bespoke requests that were never priced in. And some clients, the more you service them the more they ask for. You need to understand the point at which extras need to become chargeable.

Ask regularly: "Are we spending $1.20 to earn $1.00 on this?"

3. Re-work & Warranty Cost

Nothing eats margin quite like paying for yesterday's work all over again. A spike in re-work or warranty claims is basically your P&L waving a red flag. What's more, client satisfaction erodes, and once they have spotted one issue, they are statistically likely to spot many more. Re-work breeds re-work, and can be a slow drip of profit leakage for many organisations.

4. Overtime & Churn

Excess overtime and rising turnover aren't just HR issues - they're financial warning signs. And not just because of the overtime bill. Burnout today becomes recruitment costs, training costs and quality problems tomorrow. Not to mention the organisational knowledge loss of churn. You pay for poorly managed overtime and churn for many years after the event.

5. Cash-Flow Timing

A healthy P&L can still sink if cash comes in too slowly. Late-paying clients or long billing cycles quietly strangle growth and spike stress for everyone. Slow payments in often leads to slow payments out, and this can erode your downstream relationships too. Cash is King, because without it (even in a profitable business) the whole ecosystem dies.

Leader's Takeaway:

You don't need to own the spreadsheet, but you do need to know which of these needles moves when you or your team make a decision. A quick monthly glance at these five beats a 50-slide rainbow KPI pack any day.

Profit-savvy leaders keep these signals in view so they can spot leaks early - before they become "urgent cost-cutting initiatives" announced at 4:59 p.m. on a Thursday.

Talking Profit Upwards: Boards, Executives & Budget Battles

Plenty of smart mid-level leaders lose influence with the executive team or the board because they present their needs in the wrong language. They talk about feelings and fairness; the board hears "cost centre asking for more money." That's not to say Boards don't care. The opposite is true of many of the Boards we work with where they care almost too deeply at times. However, a Board's primary role is a duty to the organisation, and so they must be focused on the levers that protect the business.

If you want the decision-makers to back your team's needs - whether it's more headcount, new tools or just protecting a budget line - you have to link it to the levers they care about: risk, cost, growth, return.

1. Lead with the Business Impact

Skip the back-story about how hard everyone's been working; start with the business stakes.

"If we don't fund this upgrade, downtime will cost an estimated $X per month."

"An extra hire reduces overtime by 20 %, saving $Y and lowering burnout risk."

It's not about emotionless spreadsheets - it's about framing your ask in terms of what they already want to protect and aligning with that need.

2. Show the Trade-Offs

Boards know there's no free lunch.

Help them see the choice:

"We can keep delaying recruitment and keep paying for contractor overtime, or invest in one permanent role that pays for itself in six months."

This shifts the conversation from "Please give us money" to "Here's the smarter investment."

3. Bring a Risk Lens

Executives and boards respond fast to risk: reputational, legal, safety, customer churn.

- "Cutting this budget risks losing two key clients worth $X annually."
- "Not addressing this hazard now increases the likelihood of compensation claims."

Risk often unlocks action faster than a line-item saving.

4. Avoid the Jargon Olympics

Slinging acronyms (or initialism for the picky) back and forth just creates a contest no one wins. Plain language lands better than buzz-word bingo - especially when half the room secretly doesn't know the acronym either. Speak in concise, easy to understand, real-world language if you want to be heard.

5. Close with the Win

Make the upside clear: shorter lead-times, higher margin, reduced turnover, happier customers.

Paint the picture of what success looks like in metrics and in human terms.

Leader's Takeaway:

Influence upwards isn't about being the loudest voice; it's about making the business case so clear the decision almost makes itself. The better you are at linking your team's needs to the organisation's Profit levers, the easier it is to get the right resources - without the boardroom melodrama.

Reflection Corner – Your Profit Pulse Check

Grab a pen or the back of last month's budget print-out (it's probably still sitting on your desk).

Rate yourself on a scale of 1-5.

1 = Needs work   3 = Passable   5 = Rock-solid

Profit Basics

- I understand how my team's work connects to the organisation's main value drivers (revenue, cost, risk, customer value).
- I keep an eye on at least three core profit signals - margin, cost-to-serve, re-work, overtime/churn or cash-flow timing.
- I can explain those numbers in plain English to my team.

Money Conversations

- I regularly link budget decisions to trade-offs and priorities, not just "we can't afford it."
- I can frame a business case for more resources that shows return or risk-reduction - not just a plea for help.
- I share wins when the team saves money or grows margin so they see their impact.

Profit Myths & Habits

- I challenge the "more revenue fixes everything" myth when I see it.
- I don't over-service favourite customers for free.
- I cut waste, not essentials - and I explain the difference.

Circle your lowest-scoring cluster. That's where profit is probably sneaking out the back door.

Write down one small move you'll make this week to plug a leak - kill a zombie project, fix a cost-to-serve black hole, or finally have that budget conversation with the boss.

Closing

Profit isn't about turning leaders into accountants or stripping the soul out of the work. It's about making sure the lights stay on so the mission can keep going. It's about sparing your team the chaos and jerk-style panic that comes from poor financial decisions.

When you understand the levers and talk about them openly and confidently, you stop being the "budget victim" and become a partner in the organisation's success. That's the kind of leadership that gets noticed (and funded).

Even with the three pillars in place, pressure, change and sheer fatigue can pull any of us back toward the jerk-zone. In the next section we'll bring the three pillars together - People, Proficiency and Profit - and show how to keep all three in balance so you don't drift back into Dormant, Distant or Disaster leadership territory.

CHAPTER 6

STAYING OUT OF
THE THREE D'S

"The Jerk Is Always Lurking"

The truth about leadership is this: in this life, you never graduate from being human.

No matter how polished your skills, the slide back into Dormant, Distant or Disaster mode (and Jerkdom) is always just a bad week away. One rough quarter, a sleepless fortnight, a new boss with an urgent obsession, or that endless budget squeeze.

Stress shortens tempers. Pressure squeezes out empathy. Deadlines crowd out the habits that kept you steady. That's not moral failure - it's gravity and inertia. Left unchecked, it pulls even the best leaders off-centre.

A CEP Cancels Mid-Session

Halfway through a leadership session - thirty people engaged, markers squeaking, real progress - a new CEO walked in. No hello. No context. "We're restructuring," he announced, "and this program is cancelled." Then he left. I discovered my own contract had been terminated at the same time the participants did.

This was the same CEO who fired a long-serving COO while she was on maternity leave. Technically legal (apparently), morally repellent, strategically foolish. You could feel the oxygen leave the room. People looked at the floor. A few laughed - the brittle, awkward kind. One person asked if they should stop the exercise. We did. Coffee never tasted so bitter.

What's the lesson? Not that leaders shouldn't make hard calls. It's how you make them - and how you carry the humans through. A one-paragraph email that nukes trust is not "decisive leadership." It's cowardice disguised as urgency.

The jerk switch here was pressure. New leaders want to prove control. The Profit pillar was screaming (or so he thought), so he bulldozed People and Proficiency - exactly how you slide into Disaster or Distant leadership. He got none of the benefits of change (because the team quietly resisted everything after that) and all of the costs (attrition, shadow sabotage, vendor relationships torched for sport).

A month later, a senior manager confided: "We didn't need the whole program to continue. We needed the respect of being told like adults." That sentence could be engraved above the doorway of half the change failures we see.

"Tuesday with Tania"

Tania*, a mid-level manager we'd coached two years earlier, had nailed her People pillar - high trust, engaged team - and her Proficiency pillar - smooth processes, no drama.

Then came a high-stakes product launch: ten-hour days of back-to-back meetings, the CFO demanding weekly cost-saving reports, and two senior team members going on parental leave within weeks of each other.

Within a month she was living in her inbox, cancelling one-on-ones and snapping at people in meetings. By quarter-end, her once-loyal team was avoiding her in the hallway.

Tania hadn't turned into a jerk overnight. Under Profit pressure and delivery demands, she'd let the People pillar slide - tipping her into Distant Leader mode, where the work and numbers still got done but the humans felt abandoned.

The point: regression is normal - but preventable. Each of the pillars in the Dynamic Leader model house a variety of skills. These skills need to be practiced and honed on-goingly. There is no destination on this leadership journey - it is a continuum. If we don't keep our muscles strong in each of the pillars, when the pressure comes every one of us would fall back into Jerk territory.

This chapter will show you how to:

- Spot early warning signs that one pillar is slipping.

- Run a quick self-check when the heat's on.
- Reset fast before you do serious damage to people, profit or your own sanity.

Reading the Dashboard – Early Warning Signs You're Slipping

Even the best leaders don't wake up one morning as a Dormant, Distant or Disaster boss.

It creeps up on you like a slow software bug: a few skipped check-ins here, a new "urgent" deadline there, a little more snapping and a little less listening.

Here's how to spot the drift early - before your team starts dodging you in the hallway.

When the People Pillar is Slipping

- You're cancelling one-on-ones more often than keeping them.
- Team members start coming to you only for sign-offs, not for ideas.
- You realise you don't know how some of them are really doing at work or at home.
- The grapevine suddenly knows more than you do.

When the Proficiency Pillar is Slipping

- Priorities change weekly and no one can name the top three.
- Meetings end without clear owners or deadlines.
- Projects drag on; the zombie ones seem to multiply.

- You're firefighting things that used to run on rails.

When the Profit Pillar is Slipping

- You can't explain why margin is dipping or overtime is climbing.
- You're saying yes to things that don't add value because they're "urgent" or politically popular.
- Cost-to-serve on a few customers quietly creeps up but no one is watching.
- Finance is asking questions you can't answer.

Reset Rituals – How to Pull Yourself Back to Centre

Spotting the drift is half the battle. The other half is pulling yourself back before you do permanent damage - to your team, the work, or your own reputation. Or indeed your own sanity and enjoyment of work.

These "reset rituals" aren't magic. They're small, repeatable habits that keep you anchored when pressure tries to tip you back into one of the D's.

1. The Ten-Minute Audit

Once a week (Friday lunch, Monday morning - whenever you'll actually do it), ask yourself:

- Which pillar have I neglected this week?
- Where did I spend most of my energy: People, Proficiency or Profit?
- What suffered because of it?

Jot the answers down. The goal isn't guilt - it's awareness.

2. One-to-One Triage

If the People pillar is wobbling, start with the humans:

- Re-book any one-on-ones you cancelled.
- Walk the floor or ping the hybrid team on chat - not to check up, but to check in.
- Pick one relationship that feels "off" and reconnect.

Often the act of showing up resets half the People damage. When people see you trying to change for the better, more often than not they will give you some space to make mistakes.

3. The White-Board Reset

If Proficiency has slipped:

- Grab a whiteboard (or a blank doc) and list the top three priorities.
- Park everything else on a "Not-Now" list.
- Close every open meeting today with: "Who's doing what by when?"

This gets the chaos back into containers.

4. The 15-Minute Money Huddle

If Profit feels blurry:

- Sit down with Finance or your trusted numbers-person.
- Ask three questions: Where are we winning? Where are we leaking? What's coming up next quarter?

- Share one relevant insight with your team so they see the link between their work and the dollars.

5. The Micro-Apology

If you've snapped, over-reacted, or let something slide, own it out loud:

"I dropped the ball on that update last week. I'm sorry - here's how we'll fix it."

A two-sentence apology rebuilds more trust than a ten-slide deck ever will.

6. Ritualise the Reset

Block a recurring 15-minute "DLPA check-in" on your calendar. No emails, no calls - just a weekly self-scan of People, Proficiency, Profit. Think of it as your leadership maintenance appointment.

Leader's Takeaway:

You don't need a heroic transformation - just consistent micro-resets that stop drift becoming default. When you make these resets routine, you stay in the Dynamic Leader zone instead of being dragged back into jerk-mode by stress or deadlines.

Final Reflection – Keeping All Three Pillars Standing

Leadership isn't a medal you earn once and polish on the mantelpiece. It's more like juggling flaming torches on a moving train: the second you stop paying attention, one hits the floor.

The Dynamic Leader model is your map:

People – lead humans first; trust, fairness, inclusion.

Proficiency – organise the work so things get done without chaos.

Profit – understand the commercial levers that keep the mission funded.

Drop any one of those and gravity drags you back toward Dormant, Distant or Disaster leadership.

Your Quick DLPA Pulse Check

Grab a page in your notebook and rate each pillar from 1 (Needs Work) to 5 (Rock-Solid):

People: Do I know how my team is actually doing, not just their KPIs?

Proficiency: Can my team name our top three priorities without checking a deck?

Profit: Can I explain to a new starter how what we do, connects to the dollars (or the mission) that keep the lights on?

Circle your lowest score.

That's your next workout zone.

One Move at a Time

You don't have to fix all three pillars overnight. Pick one small, visible action this week:

- Re-book that skipped one-on-one.
- Kill a zombie project.
- Share one real profit insight with your team.

Small moves compound over time. Tiny, boring discipline is what keeps big, shiny disasters at bay.

In Closing

Staying in the Dynamic Leader zone isn't about being perfect or heroic. It's about noticing when the balance wobbles and making the micro-adjustments before you end up the boss everyone avoids in the hallway, the kitchen and even the bathroom (I actually had a client where people hid in the stalls!).

If you keep the three pillars in sight and keep flexing those muscles, you won't just avoid being a jerk - you'll build a team that's engaged, productive, and commercially sharp enough to survive whatever the next curveball throws at you.

That's the point of this whole book:

Lead people well, get stuff done without drama, and keep the lights on - so the work (and the humans doing it) actually thrive.

Up until now you've heard the stories and the scars. In Chapter 7 we turn to the research - the hard data that proves these ideas aren't soft, they are strategic.

CHAPTER 7

THE SCIENCE OF GREAT (AND TERRIBLE) LEADERSHIP

It's Not Just a Gut Feeling

You don't have to take my word for it or rely on Friday-night war stories from the office.

There's a mountain of research that proves what most of us have learned the hard way:

leaders shape the climate, and the climate shapes the numbers.

The Brain on Bad Bosses

Your brain isn't magic - it's wired with ancient survival circuitry. Understanding a little neurobiology helps explain why bad leadership feels worse than it is.

The Stress Circuit: When Leadership Becomes Threat

Picture your brain as two parts:

- Prefrontal Cortex - the "executive suite" for planning, logic, empathy

- Amygdala - the "watchtower," scanning for threats (real or perceived)

When your amygdala detects danger - whether a howling tiger or a surprise "We need to talk" email - it triggers cortisol release. That floods your system and suppresses prefrontal functioning. You think less clearly, resist less, snap more.

Multiple studies show this:

Social-evaluative threat (being judged or watched) can elevate cortisol significantly, impair working memory and reduce cognitive flexibility. (Dickerson & Kemeny, 2004)

Interruptions and task-switching have been shown to degrade performance accuracy and increase error rates (Mark, Gudith & Klocke, 2008).

Multiple studies show workers exposed to frequent unpredictable interruptions report increased mental workload and reduced performance, especially when juggling complex tasks.

In short: chaos, ambiguity and unpredictable leadership spikes stress. Stress makes people worse at thinking - exactly when clear thinking matters.

Leadership Behavior as a System Trigger

When leaders shift priorities without warning, cancel commitment meetings, send cryptic emails or publicly criticise someone they aren't just being jerkish. They're activating threat systems across the team.

The vulnerability lies in modern work:

- Decisions often lack visibility, so employees fill the gaps with worst-case assumptions.
- Remote or hybrid teams reduce nonverbal cues, amplifying ambiguity.
- High-stakes goals + tight timelines + low buffer = constant threat-mode.

Behavior that might seem "tough leadership" is actually sending continual micro-shocks through people's nervous systems.

What Good Leadership Does Differently

If you want brains working - not melting - here's how to lead differently:

- Predictability & clarity: remove ambiguity so threat circuits stay quiet
- Transparent decision-making: even when the choice is tough, explain the why
- Psychological safety: build an environment where people can make mistakes or ask questions without being punished
- Normalise feedback & apology: when you slip, own it pub-

licly. Studies show that authenticity restores trust.

Over time, these buffers lower baseline stress, improve engagement, reduce error, and make teams more resilient.

This is why the DLPA pillars matter:

People - trust and fairness keep the alarm bells quiet.

Proficiency - clear priorities and processes reduce ambiguity.

Profit - when leaders explain the "why-for-them," uncertainty drops and brains stay online.

One of my favourite lines from a workshop participant was:

"So basically my amygdala thinks my boss is a bear?" Exactly. And no amount of resilience webinars will help if the bear keeps showing up at 4 p.m. with "urgent" last-minute demands.

The takeaway for leaders: if you want sharper decisions, fewer mistakes and less drama, don't just send people to mindfulness apps - stop being the thing that's spiking their cortisol.

And we're talking real data here, not just motivational posters and LinkedIn memes.

Here's what the science says.

1. Engagement: The 70 % Effect

Gallup's 2022 State of the Global Workplace found that managers account for around 70 % of the variance in team engagement scores. Engagement isn't a warm-fuzzy metric; Gallup's meta-analysis of

100k+ teams shows those in the top quartile of engagement deliver about 23% higher profitability, 18 % higher sales, and 10 % higher customer ratings, while absenteeism and quality defects drop.

When the People pillar is strong - trust, clarity, inclusion - engagement rises, and so do results.

2. Burnout & Psychosocial Hazards

WHO's ICD-11 (2019) officially recognises burnout as an "occupational phenomenon" caused by chronic workplace stress that isn't successfully managed.

Regulators such as Safe Work Australia (2023) list common psychosocial hazards: high job demands, low role-clarity or control, poor support, unfair treatment and harmful leadership behaviour. These risks have been getting more and more airtime globally, and particularly in Australia, as legislation clarifies the positive duty on employers, and regulators respond to the changing work landscape.

These conditions correlate with higher rates of anxiety, depression, workers' compensation claims and long-term absence.

Translation: if your Proficiency pillar is weak (unclear priorities, chaotic processes) or your People pillar is neglected (low trust, unfairness), you're not just stressing people out, you're generating measurable business risk.

Denial and Reputational Risk

A quick sidebar for two stories about denial and reputational risk.

No Imminent Threat to Risk

We were brought into a medical group after a string of behaviour complaints. Not clinical errors - human errors: belittling in corridors, sarcastic "banter" that wasn't, public shaming in meetings that made grown professionals tear up in their cars at lunch.

We ran interviews and anonymised them. Patterns jumped off the page: high demand + low control, inconsistent support from seniors, a few "untouchables" who behaved badly with impunity, and a change process that consisted of "email at 5 p.m. Friday." Classic psychosocial hazard constellation.

In the debrief we laid out findings. The executives - several named in multiple stories - listened politely. Then one said, with real relief, "So... no imminent threat to WHS?"

Technically, no one was about to be crushed by a falling MRI. But the frame was wrong. The question wasn't "Will anyone die today?" It was "Are we running a system that injures people over months and makes mistakes more likely?" That's what psychosocial risk is: not immediate catastrophe, but slow injury and error-prone conditions.

We shifted the conversation: here's the risk, here's how it shows up on your P&L (overtime, turnover, re-work), here's what you can fix by Thursday. Role clarity. Model a "no surprises" rule. Train middle leaders to run proper 1:1s. De-idolise the "untouchables", enforce behaviour trumps brilliance. Treat change like a people-project: context before content, pilot, feedback loops.

They didn't turn into a utopia overnight, but the snide comments faded. The weekly 1:1s surfaced two real workload constraints that were quietly breaking people. A senior scientist publicly apologised for a blow-up. That one apology did more to reset the culture than three town halls.

We Just Wanted a Good News Story

A national organisation asked us to assess their psychosocial risks. Not a tick-the-box audit - a real look under the hood: workload spikes, role confusion, support levels, how change was handled, whether people felt safe raising concerns. We interviewed across levels, ran focus groups, and reviewed data. We found exactly what you'd expect in a system that prized speed and silence: chronic high demand, low control, sporadic support, poor communication and a DIY approach to change that created more stress than progress.

We wrote a plain-English report with a very boring title (because boring is what actually gets approved), three major risks, five quick wins, and a ninety-day plan. In the readout, an executive smiled and said, "Thanks. We were actually hoping for a good-news story."

We explained the good news was the plan. The hazards weren't immutable laws - they were fixable design choices. They wanted the adjectives changed, the language softened. "Could we say 'emerging' instead of 'high'?" Could we soften "role conflict" to "role opportunity"? They wanted a branding exercise for risk.

We declined. The CEO went quiet. For ten seconds nobody breathed. Then one of the operational leaders cleared her throat. "I'd rather know the truth and get moving than have another glossy report."

She saved the day. The ninety-day plan was approved. They killed a zombie project, installed a weekly priority review, re-trained managers on basic 1:1s and feedback, and changed the change process (ironically) to treat change like a people-project. Six months later the pulse survey bumped. Not a miracle - evidence.

The lesson? The science doesn't need spin. If you're serious about psychosocial safety, your comms should be calm, transparent and adult. Ask: "Where is the work design hurting people, and what will we change first?" If the first response is, "Can the report sound happier?" you don't have a hazard problem, you have a leadership one.

Whilst psychosocial hazards can seem intimidating, and the legal landscape can seem tough to keep up with, the science gives us a robust framework, and the people give us a reason to do better. We are seeing more and more that reputation can be absolutely destroyed with one notice from the regulator being publicised. Despite the natural reflex to want to polish the turd, the braver choice of trying to really engineer a better system that minimises the risks is now also the commercially savvy one.

3. The Real Price of Turnover

The Society for Human Resource Management (SHRM) and Deloitte estimate the total cost of replacing a skilled employee - things like recruitment, lost productivity, training, ramp-up - at roughly 50 % to 200 % of that employee's annual salary.

Exit-interview data consistently rank "manager/leadership quality" among the top three reasons people leave, well ahead of pay in many sectors.

That's a six-figure drain per departure for many professional roles. And it's largely preventable with better leadership habits, and less jerks.

4. Safety, Quality & Profit

In high-risk sectors such as healthcare, Aiken et al. (2012) found that better nurse-leader support and communication correlated with fewer patient-safety incidents and lower mortality.

Zohar's "safety-climate" research in construction and manufacturing links supervisory leadership quality to lower injury and error rates. The list goes on. All of this clarifies and confirms what most workers already suspected. The better quality the leadership and communication, the less likely it is there will be an incident.

And for the pure business case for developing stronger leaders, fewer incidents = fewer claims, warranty costs and delays which is a direct boost to profit.

5. Myths the Data Kills

"Tough leaders get the best results."

Research shows command-and-control styles may spike short-term output but undermine engagement, innovation and retention within 12-18 months.

"Soft skills don't pay the bills."

Gallup's meta-analysis shows teams with strong relationships, trust and clarity outperform on both profit and customer loyalty.

"Change fatigue is inevitable."

McKinsey's Organizing for Successful Change (2015) found organisations that invest in change-communication and staff support are about 3× more likely to hit their transformation goals.

Closing the Loop

The evidence is remarkably consistent across sectors and decades and geographies:

Better leadership = better wellbeing = better performance.

The DLPA model lines up neatly with the science:

- People Pillar reduces psychosocial hazards and lifts engagement.
- Proficiency Pillar lowers workload stress and error rates.
- Profit Pillar connects effort to outcomes so people see meaning and value in their work.

Leaders who keep all three pillars in balance aren't just nicer to work for, they're statistically better for the bottom line.

Psychosocial Hazards Demystified

The term psychosocial hazard sounds like something out of a dystopian HR manual.

In reality, it just means the way we organise work can harm people's mental health, safety or performance and often it's totally fixable.

What the Regulators Actually Mean

Safe Work Australia's 2022 Code of Practice and the international ISO 45003 guideline list a familiar set of culprits. Here are the big ones you'll recognise from any busy workplace:

- High or chronic job demand – relentless workload, constant urgency, no recovery time.

- Low role clarity / role conflict – either no one knows who owns what, or two people think they both do.

- Low control / autonomy – every small decision needs five approvals.

- Poorly-managed change & uncertainty – priorities lurch around, new systems drop in with no warning.

- Unfairness / low organisational justice – obvious favouritism, promotions by politics not merit.

- Low support from leaders or peers – feeling abandoned when things go wrong.

- Remote or isolated work without connection – out-of-sight becomes out-of-mind.

- Bullying, harassment or toxic behaviour – sadly still alive and well in too many offices and organisations.

None of these are mysteries; they're management choices. If they're ignored, they become stress triggers, drive disengagement and, in Australia and many other jurisdictions, become a legal compliance risk.

Why Leaders Should Care (Beyond the Law)

Numerous meta-analyses and large reviews show that high demands, low control (autonomy), poor support and unclear roles are among the strongest predictors of burnout over time.

While precise percentages vary by study and context, the consistent finding is that structural work factors - not personal weakness - drive much of the risk.

And reputationally?

In an age where a single regulator notice or viral Glassdoor review can torch a brand's credibility, hoping no one notices is not a strategy.

DLPA *Lens* on Hazards

- People pillar tamps down unfairness, isolation and poor support.
- Proficiency pillar fixes role clarity, change chaos and workload management.
- Profit pillar reduces panic and conflicting priorities by connecting work to strategy.

When one pillar collapses, hazards spike.

Leader's Quick-Scan for Hazards

Tick what applies to your team this quarter:

- We've had three or more "all-hands, drop everything" crises in the past month.

- Key roles or priorities still lack clear owners.
- Team members can't adjust deadlines without climbing two rungs of hierarchy.
- We've launched change in the last six months with little notice or training.
- Two or more people think promotion decisions aren't fair or transparent.
- New starters say onboarding felt like "sink or swim."
- Remote staff say they feel out of the loop.
- Behaviour that breaches our values has been ignored or excused.

One or two ticks: probably normal growing pains.

Three or more: you've got active psychosocial risks worth tackling before they tackle you.

Closing Note

Whilst psychosocial hazards can feel like a legal mine-field, the science is just describing the conditions for good work: clarity, control, fairness, support and respect. Get those right and you're not only on the right side of the law - you're unlocking better performance and loyalty.

Science in Practice - Monday Morning Mojo

The data is great for board packs and TED slides. But here's what it actually means at 9 a.m. on Monday when you've got a meeting, two unread emails marked urgent, and a team that's already on caffeine drip-feed.

1. Turn Engagement into a Habit

Why: Gallup says your (yes *your*) behaviour drives 70 % of the engagement swings.

Do: Keep one standing 1:1 per person each fortnight and don't bump it for "urgent" stuff. It doesn't need to go for an hour. Fifteen minutes is often enough if it's focused, not rushed.

Impact: Early fixes for small issues before they morph into turnover and quality dips.

2. Protect Role Clarity

Why: "Low role-clarity" is a named and known psychosocial hazard. And one of the easier ones to fix.

Do: Once a quarter, run a 30-minute "who-owns-what" check-in. Role clarity isn't just about my own role, it's clarity about other people's roles as well, and where they intersect.

Impact: Cuts stress, reduces re-work, keeps people out of blame-ping-pong.

3. Measure a Human Metric Next to a Business Metric

Why: Burnout hides until it's expensive.

Do: Add one wellbeing signal (like overtime hours or unplanned absences) next to every delivery KPI you review.

Impact: Early warning before you burn out staff and budget. The human signals will often tell you what's about to happen to the financial ones.

4. Close the Loop on Change

Why: McKinsey's 3× success stat on change projects.

Do: End every change update with "Here's what stays the same, here's who to ask if it feels clunky or confusing."

Impact: Calms brains, reduces resistance, speeds adoption. Create safety in what is remaining the same, and excitement (and clarity) about what is changing.

5. Celebrate Value-Adders Out Loud

Why: People repeat what gets noticed.

Do: Give a quick shout-out when a smart process tweak saves time, re-work or dollars. Make sure you frame as value adds, and not just senseless cost cutting.

Impact: Builds a culture that protects both people and profit.

Leader's takeaway:

You don't need a research degree to use the science. Small, predictable rituals like the weekly check-in, the extra line on the KPI sheet, the two-sentence context in a change meeting, add up to big shifts in engagement, safety, quality and margin.

Insight is great and a necessary first step, but only action changes the lived reality. Chapter 8 is your grab-and-go toolkit to get started: checklists, scripts and quick-hit practices you can drop straight into daily work.

CHAPTER 8

THE DYNAMIC LEADER TOOLKIT

"Because leadership needs better tools than another motivational poster."

Leadership shouldn't feel like improv theatre, and yet that's how most of us learn it: make it up, hope it lands, apologise later. Fake it till you make it.

The DLPA pillars gave you the 'what' to focus on. This chapter gives you the how - practical tools you can pull out on a Tuesday afternoon when the wheels are wobbling.

Think of it as your field-kit: a mix of templates, check-lists, questions, and habits.

Some will take you 10 minutes. Some you can run as a team huddle.

All of them are designed to lower drama, raise clarity, and keep you out of jerk-territory.

How to Use This Chapter

Don't try to deploy all the tools at once - that's the fastest route to overwhelm (and ironically, more drama).

Skim the tools, mark the one that solves today's pain-point, start there. Then build the habits gradually - the goal is to make them routine, not a side-project.

Tool 1: The Psychosocial Hazard Spotter

You can't manage what you can't see - and psychosocial stress is often invisible until it hits the sick-leave register or workers compensation.

A huge chunk of "bad culture" complaints come down to unmanaged psychosocial hazards - things at work that quietly erode mental health and performance. This tool helps you spot them before they turn into burnout, conflict or a claim.

The 5 Fast-Check Hazards

At your next team meeting or one-on-one, run your eye across these five areas. Tick any that are present. If you tick two or more, you've probably got a hazard that needs attention.

THE 5 FAST-CHECK HAZARDS	
High Demand + Low Control	Are deadlines relentless and people feel they have no say in how to meet them?
Unclear Roles	Are there regular "I thought you were doing that" moments, or the same task done twice?
Low Support / High Friction	Do people hesitate to ask for help because they fear being labelled "not coping"?
Unpredictable Change	Are priorities or processes shifting weekly with little explanation?
Perceived Un-fairness	Do people believe favourites get the plum work or that decisions are opaque? Are there two sets of rules at play?

Spotter Questions for Leaders

Use these in skip-levels, pulse-checks or informal chats:

- "What's the hardest part of your week right now?"
- "What's one thing that would make this job easier tomorrow?"
- "Where do we waste the most energy?"
- "If you were in my seat, what's the first change you'd make for the team's wellbeing?"

What to Do Next

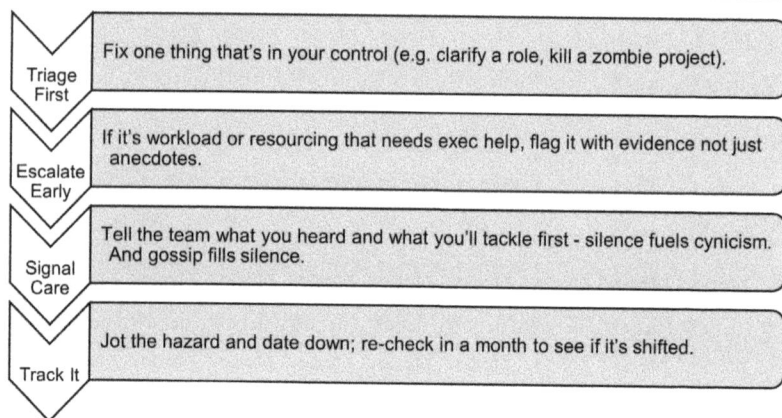

Triage First	Fix one thing that's in your control (e.g. clarify a role, kill a zombie project).
Escalate Early	If it's workload or resourcing that needs exec help, flag it with evidence not just anecdotes.
Signal Care	Tell the team what you heard and what you'll tackle first - silence fuels cynicism. And gossip fills silence.
Track It	Jot the hazard and date down; re-check in a month to see if it's shifted.

Psychosocial safety isn't just HR policy; it's daily housekeeping by every leader.

Tool 2: The 1-on-1 Cheat-Sheet: Stop Winging It

A good 1-on-1 is like flossing - everyone swears they do it regularly, but the dentist (or the engagement survey) knows the truth.

Most leaders run their one-on-ones like last-minute improv: "Sooo... how's everything going?" followed by awkward small-talk and a quick calendar reshuffle for 'something urgent'.

Bad one-on-ones waste time; skipped ones breed drama. Here's the simple cheat-sheet to make them count.

The 15-Minute Frame

A 30-minute slot works best, but you only need 15 solid minutes of actual conversation.

Break it into three quick beats:

THREE QUICK BEATS	
Work	"What's going well / what's stuck?"
Humans	"How's your energy / what's making work harder than it needs to be?"
Future	"Any skills or opportunities you want to chase?"

That's it. Stop talking. Let them fill the silence. Silence is where the real gold lives.

GROUND RULES	
Show up on time	Nothing says "you don't matter" like the boss breezing in seven minutes late with a latte.
Phones down, email closed	Otherwise, you're just running a distracted scroll-and-tell.
Capture actions	A sticky note, a text to yourself, a magic spreadsheet... just something.
Close with clarity	"Here's what I'll do, here's what I need from you by Friday."
And critically: Follow through	The commitments made are only as good as the follow through and the accountability which follows. Otherwise, it's just another empty chat and time suck.

If you regularly cancel or drift through 1-on-1s, stop wondering why small issues turn into full-blown HR sagas. Try this simple framework and see the difference.

Tool 3: Feedback Without the Flinch

If the only feedback your team gets is at the annual review, you're not giving feedback - you're doing autopsies.

Leaders dodge feedback because they think it has to be a dramatic sit-down, complete with tissues, diagrams and maybe a priest. It doesn't. Short, frequent and specific is the secret.

The 2-Minute Loop

Use this any time you spot a behaviour worth repeating (or stopping):

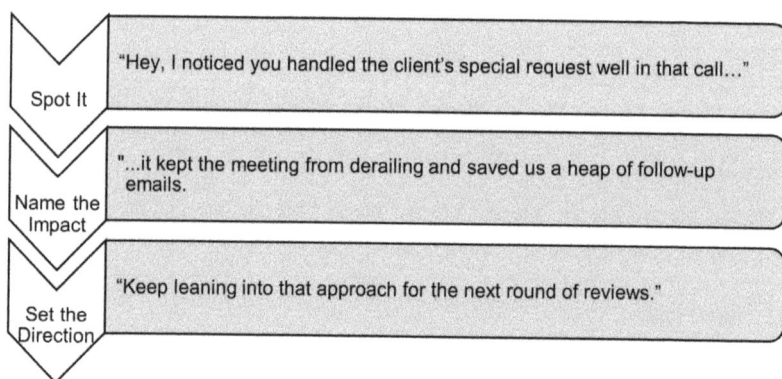

Spot It	"Hey, I noticed you handled the client's special request well in that call..."
Name the Impact	"...it kept the meeting from derailing and saved us a heap of follow-up emails.
Set the Direction	"Keep leaning into that approach for the next round of reviews."

Positive or corrective, same formula. No drama, no lecture.

For Tough Stuff – The O.I.E.S. Frame

THE O.I.E.S. FRAME	
Observation	"I noticed the last two reports were late."
Impact	"That pushed the testing team behind schedule."

Expectation	"We need those in by Wednesday, so the rest of the process stays on track."
Support	"What would help you hit the deadline next week?"

Short, respectful, human. Also harder for the other person to argue with facts than with your feelings.

And remember, the easiest way to show your team that feedback isn't scary is to be open to it yourself. Mic drop.

Pro-Tip

Ask for feedback back: "Anything I could have done differently to make that project easier for you?"

The first few times they'll say "Nah, all good," because they don't believe you mean it.

Keep asking until they start telling you the truth.

Feedback given and received regularly shrinks psychosocial hazards like 'unfairness' and 'low support' before they metastasise.

Tool 4: The Priority Parking Lot

If everything's Priority 1, nothing's actually moving - except maybe your blood pressure.

Most teams have a To-Do list that looks like the warehouse scene in Raiders of the Lost Ark, endless shelves of Important Stuff that nobody can find or finish. The cure? A simple Parking Lot.

How It Works

THE PRIORITY PARKING LOT	
Pick a Maximum of 3 Active Priorities.	Yes, just three. Your brain (and your calendar) will thank you.
Park the Rest.	Everything else goes to the Parking Lot board. It's not gone, it's just... not invited to dinner right now.
Review Weekly.	Move things in or out only if something genuinely more valuable arrives or one of the three gets done.

Why It Works

- Shrinks the chaos and decision-fatigue.

- Makes trade-offs visible to everyone - no more mystery about why Project X stalled.

- Builds trust because people finally see what's actually important this week.

Your Parking Lot is the most underrated psychosocial-hazard control you'll ever use. It kills "priority confetti" and stops the hamster wheel from turning into a blender.

Tool 5: The Anti-Drama Meeting Kit

A bad meeting is like a bad sequel - too long, nothing happens, and you wish you had at least bought popcorn.

Most meetings are long because nobody prepped, unclear because nobody knows the goal, and pointless because nothing changes afterwards.

Here's the kit to save your Fridays (and your will to live).

THE ANTI-DRAMA MEETING KIT		
Pre-Meeting	The 3-Sentence Test	If you can't write the meeting's purpose in three plain-language sentences, you're not ready to meet.
During the Meeting	Ban the Slide-Reading	Send decks in advance. Meeting time is for discussion, not audiobook theatre.
	Use a Live Action List	Visible to all, if there's no action, there's no meeting. Close each topic with: "Who's doing what by when?"
	The 25-Minute Rule	The default meeting slot is 25 minutes. Anything longer needs a really impactful purpose (and measurable outcome.

THE ANTI-DRAMA MEETING KIT		
Post-Meeting	Action Focus	Share the action list only - not a novella of minutes nobody will read. Re-cap in the next meeting what got done (or didn't). That's your accountability loop.

Remember, if the only thing produced by your meetings is another meeting invite, congratulations: you've invented organisational purgatory.

Extra Psychosocial Bonus

Structured meetings reduce role confusion, lower constant "urgent" interruptions, and give people back focus time which are all known hazard reducers.

Tool 6: Profit-Signals Radar

Profit rarely disappears overnight. It leaks out in drips while everyone's too busy polishing dashboards to notice.

Most leaders don't need to build the budget spreadsheet themselves, but they do need to spot when the unit they lead is quietly eating margin or funding somebody else's overtime habit.

5 Profit Signals Worth Watching

(You don't need an MBA to track these - just curiosity and a notepad.)

5 PROFIT SIGNALS WORTH WATCHING	
Cost-to-Serve Drift	Jobs or customers taking longer / needing more hand-holding than planned? That's margin walking out the door.
Re-Work & Do-Overs	If you're fixing the same thing twice, you're paying double for the same outcome.
Scope Creep That Never Creeps Back	"While you're at it..." is the silent profit killer. If you don't log and price the extras, you're basically donating free labour.
Overtime & Burnout Hours	If the same few people are clocking heroic hours, you're propping up a broken system and risking churn.
Churn in Your Best People or Customers	When your best performers leave or your best clients stop re-ordering, the profit hit shows up three months later, not immediately.

How to Run the Radar

Do a monthly 20-minute huddle with Finance or Ops to eyeball these five areas.

Pick one leak to plug each month. Don't boil the ocean.

Share the headline trend with your team - they'll often have the fastest fixes hiding in plain sight.

Profit isn't only the CFO's hobby; it's everyone's business. If the lights go out, the coffee machine goes with it.

Tool 7: Useful-Metrics Cheat-Sheet

If the only thing you're measuring is speed, don't be shocked when quality and people fall apart trying to keep up.

The right metrics steer behaviour; the wrong ones fuel drama. This cheat-sheet keeps leaders focused on impact, not vanity.

Three Buckets That Matter

THREE BUCKETS THAT MATTER	
Flow Metrics – Is the work moving or stuck?	Lead-time, cycle-time, on-time delivery, blocker-clearance time.
Quality Metrics – Is it any good the first time?	Error rate, re-work volume, first-time-right %, customer complaints.
Capacity & Health Metrics – Can the humans keep this up?	Overtime hours, unplanned absenteeism, re-grettable turnover, EAP or wellness-program uptake.

Red-Flag Patterns

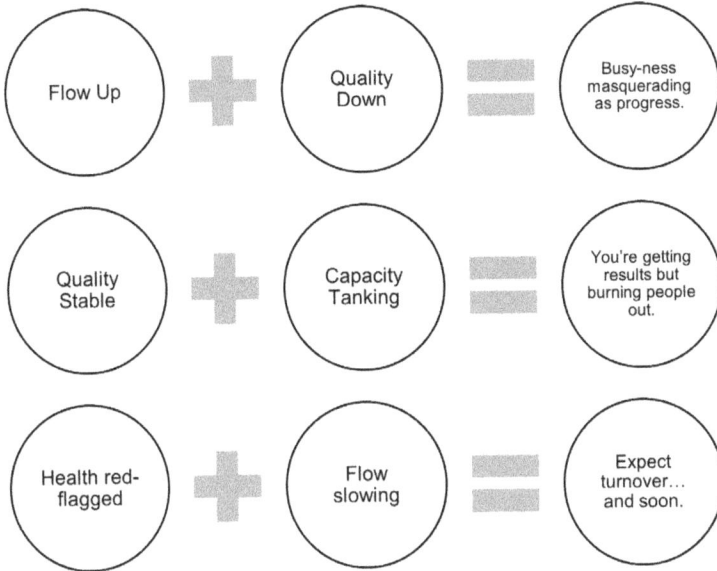

Flow Up	+	Quality Down	=	Busy-ness masquerading as progress.
Quality Stable	+	Capacity Tanking	=	You're getting results but burning people out.
Health red-flagged	+	Flow slowing	=	Expect turnover... and soon.

Psychosocial Safety Link

Balanced metrics send the message: "We care about results and keeping humans in one piece."

That alone lowers stress, perceived unfairness and churn.

Wrap-Up: From Tool to Culture

You now have more tools than a late-night infomercial: check-lists, cheat-sheets, hazard spotters, meeting hacks, and enough one-liners to survive most Monday mornings.

But remember: a tool in a drawer fixes nothing. (That's not slang for anything for anyone of my generation. I mean like a screwdriver).

Leaders don't change culture with a laminated checklist. They change it by using the checklist every Tuesday, until it stops feeling like a checklist and just feels like "how we work here."

THREE GOLDEN RULES FOR MAKING THE TOOLS STICK	
1. Start with One Pain-Point, Not Ten	Pick the tool that solves the thing that's wrecking your week right now.
	Parking Lot a few priorities?
	A decent 1-on-1 routine?
	Use it, nail it, then add the next.
2. Use the Tools Out Loud	Tell your team: "Here's the new way we're going to run 1-on-1s" or "Let's try a weekly hazard check-in."
	Being transparent makes the habit visible and contagious.
3. Review, Don't Abandon	Block ten minutes each month to ask:
	"Which of these habits is still serving us? Which one have we quietly ghosted, and do we need it back?"

Final Nudge

These aren't quick-fix gimmicks. They're the daily habits that shrink psychosocial hazards, calm the chaos, and give your team a fighting chance to be brilliant without you hovering.

The more you practise them, the less jerk-like you'll feel on your worst day - and the less your team will want to divert you to voicemail.

Tools help you solve today's problems, but leadership is always moving and adapting. In Chapter 9 we look at the shifts already reshaping work. Things like AI, hybrid and remote working, new expectations of wellbeing, different social contract with work itself. And we will look at how the DLPA pillars keep leaders future-proof.

CHAPTER 9

THE FUTURE WON'T WAIT FOR BETTER BOSSES

The Fossil Boss

Picture this: it's 2035 and your Monday townhall is being live-translated into six languages by AI, your top coder lives in Lisbon, the customer-service queue is triaged by a bot called Sunny, and the office espresso machine refuses to start unless your wellbeing metrics look acceptable.

Meanwhile, there's still that one manager in the corner office who insists that the team be "back at their desks by 8:30 sharp" because he "likes to see people working". That boss is now a museum piece. The last of a species that thinks motivation means a pep-talk and an after-hours pizza night.

The future of leadership isn't coming; it's already in the building. The question is whether you'll still be relevant in it.

1. What's Really Changing (and Why It Matters)

Every generation swears the world is changing faster than ever; this time it's actually true.

The forces reshaping how we lead over the next decade are already in play:

- Hybrid & Borderless Teams Are the Default

  Talent is global. Geography is optional. Leadership can no longer be performed by "walking the floor". Many organisations don't even have a floor to walk.

- Humans + Machines, Not Humans vs. Machines

  AI, automation and digital co-workers are changing what's considered "human work".

  Leaders will be orchestrators of human judgment plus machine efficiency.

- The Deal Has Changed: Wellbeing, Purpose, Flexibility

  Post-pandemic, employees are done trading health and sanity for a steady pay-cheque.

  Flexibility and meaning have become non-negotiable currency. Work is no longer the stuff of core identity. It's important, but it's usually what I do rather than what I am.

- Workplace Safety Now Includes the Head and the Heart

  Psychosocial-hazard regulation is rising globally. Burnout and bullying aren't just bad culture anymore, they're legal liabilities.

- Data Everywhere, Clarity Nowhere

  We're drowning in dashboards but starving for insight. Leaders must filter signals from noise and stop confusing metrics with progress.

If your leadership playbook was printed before cloud-based computer was the standard and mental-health legislation were common, it's overdue for recycling.

2. Why the Old Playbook Dies Hard

Command-and-control leadership thrived in a world of factory lines, predictable markets and clear career ladders. That world is gone. We've still got the habits.

Speed vs. Control – Top-down approvals simply can't keep up with markets that change weekly. Workforces cannot move quickly enough if every move has to be approved in a bottleneck.

Productivity Theatre – Leaders still equate long hours and visible busyness with output. Hybrid work has exposed how hollow that is. Eroding productivity metrics also show the fallacy this is, as we see effort increase and productivity erode globally.

Burnout as a 'Personal Weakness' – Treating exhaustion as an individual failing instead of a system design flaw is not just cruel, it's commercially dumb.

The Lone-Hero Myth – We still lionise the charismatic boss who "saves" the business. The future belongs to teams that out-collaborate, not bosses who out-perform.

3. The DLPA Model, Future-Proofed

The good news: you don't need a new alphabet soup of frameworks.

The three DLPA pillars - People, Proficiency, Profit - still work; they just need future-tuning.

People: leading humans you may rarely meet in person, across cultures, time-zones and next to AI co-workers.

Proficiency: embedding agility, continuous learning and systems that can flex as fast as the market.

Profit: stretching beyond dollars to include sustainability, social licence and ethical tech, the new stakes in staying viable.

The leaders who can keep all three pillars balanced will be the ones still standing and thriving in ten years.

4. Five Habits of the Future-Ready Leader

1. Curiosity > Certainty

The shelf-life of expertise is shrinking. Leaders who can say "I don't know yet - let's find out fast" will out-run those clinging to old answers.

Ask more questions, test more often, retire outdated practices quicker than your competitors.

2. Psychological Safety as a Strategic Asset

In hybrid, diverse, AI-blended teams, people will only share half-formed ideas or spot early risks if they feel safe from ridicule or blame. That's not "soft"; it's the difference between innovation and expensive silence.

3. Radical Clarity

Future work is noisy: Slack, Teams, dashboards, alerts, half-heard directives. Leaders who can cut the noise - "Here's what matters this week, here's what can wait" - will preserve both focus and wellbeing.

4. Wellbeing as a Core Business Metric

Regulators now demand it, talent now expects it, the bottom-line rewards it. Designing workload like you design budgets - predictable peaks, recovery time, sustainable pace - becomes a leadership competence, not an HR perk.

5. Tech-Empathy

It's not enough to roll out a shiny tool; you have to understand how humans will react to it. Every tech rollout is also a people-project. Future-ready leaders blend digital literacy with emotional intelligence.

5. The Jerk of the Future (and How to Avoid Being One)

Tomorrow's jerk boss won't necessarily be the yeller or the micromanager. They'll be the leader who:

- Ignores wellbeing data because "everyone's fine".

- Lets AI decide workloads without human oversight.
- Expects hybrid teams to work like 1990s office dwellers.
- Drowns teams in dashboards but never explains the why.

Avoiding future-jerk status means staying human-centred while becoming tech-smart, not one or the other.

6. Call-to-Action: Practise, Don't Predict

The future of work is unpredictable; the skills for leading it aren't. Keep practising all three DLPA pillars, keep scanning the horizon, keep learning faster than the change-cycle.

Don't try to be the perfect future leader. Be the current leader who's willing to adapt faster than yesterday's boss.

Final Thought

Leadership isn't headed for extinction - bad leadership is. The next decade will reward leaders who can balance empathy with execution, curiosity with clarity, and humans with tech.

If you take nothing else from this book:

Don't lead like a jerk - now or in 2035.

Epilogue – Fewer Jerks, More Joy

Writing this book has been a little like coaching a very large room of leaders all at once, minus the coffee, plus a lot more time arguing with my laptop (and myself).

I started DLPA because I'd seen too many brilliant humans give up on leadership, or give up on themselves because they thought they weren't cut out for it. What they really lacked wasn't talent or heart; it was a simple, human-centred structure.

The DLPA model grew out of that need: a way to show that great leadership isn't magic or charisma, rather it's a set of muscles you can build and keep building.

The work still brings me joy - though at times, of course, frustration.

There's nothing quite like watching a leader who thought they were "not a people person" suddenly nail a tough conversation without breaking trust. Or seeing a team that's been stuck in fire-drill mode finally breathe because they know what matters this week and what can wait.

That spark when someone realises they can lead well and still sleep at night is why I do this.

This book has been a different kind of joy.

It forced me to distill a decade of workshops, coaching calls, coffee-fuelled late-night strategy sessions and even the occasional spectacular failure into words that (I hope) feel useful and a bit fun to read.

There were moments I laughed out loud writing a story I'd forgotten, and moments I wished I could go back and give my younger self this book before I learned some lessons the hard way.

If there's one thing I hope you take from these pages, it's that leadership done well is not a burden; it's a privilege. The privilege of shaping workplaces where people can do their best work and still have a life worth living. Where profit isn't a dirty word, proficiency isn't red tape, and the people side isn't treated like an optional extra.

My bigger hope is that together we create workplaces with fewer jerks.

Fewer leaders promoted without a map. Fewer teams crushed under drama and unclear expectations. Fewer Monday mornings where talented humans wonder if the job is worth the toll.

If you've picked up even one new habit from this book - a better one-on-one, a clearer priority list, a little more empathy under pressure - you're already part of that shift.

The DLPA journey doesn't end here.

Leadership isn't a box to tick; it's a continuum. You'll have great weeks and rough ones.

Just keep leaning back to the centre of the model - People, Proficiency, Profit - and keep practising. Every day you do is one day further away from the jerk-zone.

Thank you for reading, for leading, and for caring enough to get better at it. Here's to fewer jerks and more joy - at work and everywhere else.

All the best,

Karlie

ABOUT THE AUTHOR:

Karlie Cremin is the CEO of DLPA and Crestcom ANZ, organisations dedicated to helping businesses solve complex people challenges with practical, real-world solutions. She partners with organisations to design bespoke leadership programs, psychosocial hazard consulting, and people-focused strategies that build stronger cultures and more capable teams.

With a career spanning construction, government, not-for-profits, and the import sector, Karlie brings deep expertise in strategy, business model design, and workforce development. She is passionate about business sustainability and profitability, driven by her belief that people are the key drivers of organisational performance.

Through DLPA, Karlie has helped organisations reduce staff churn, improve engagement, strengthen decision-making, and ultimately boost business performance. Under her leadership, DLPA has received a range of prestigious awards:

Asia-Pacific Stevie Awards 2025

- Most Innovative Entrepreneur of the Year
- Innovative Achievement in Thought Leadership
- Innovative Achievement in Growth

International Business Awards 2025

- Woman of the Year
- Thought Leader of the Year
- Most Innovative Company of the Year

LEARNX Awards 2025

- Leadership Development
- Learning and Development
- Wellbeing
- Custom and Bespoke Learning

Stevie Award 2025

- Women in Business

HRD Service Provider Awards

- 2024: Human Resources Director
- 2023: Learning & Development
- 2022: Learning & Development and Talent Management
- 2019: Learning and Development

Australian Construction Awards 2019

- Women in the Construction Industry

Her focus remains on building sustainable, profitable businesses by equipping leaders and teams with the skills and tools they need to succeed.